A EULOGY TO ABSENT FRIENDS

An Indictment of Humanity since Time Immemorial

by

J. N. Slater

Grosvenor House
Publishing Limited

All rights reserved
Copyright © J. N. Slater, 2014

The right of J. N. Slater to be identified as the author of this
work has been asserted by him in accordance with Section 78
of the Copyright, Designs and Patents Act 1988

The book cover picture is copyright to J. N. Slater

This book is published by
Grosvenor House Publishing Ltd
28-30 High Street, Guildford, Surrey, GU1 3EL.
www.grosvenorhousepublishing.co.uk

This book is sold subject to the conditions that it shall not, by way of
trade or otherwise, be lent, resold, hired out or otherwise circulated
without the author's or publisher's prior consent in any form of binding or
cover other than that in which it is published and
without a similar condition including this condition being imposed
on the subsequent purchaser.

A CIP record for this book
is available from the British Library

ISBN 978-1-78148-677-1

Dedication

To humankind, and all creatures great and small that have been killed because of war.

Acknowledgements

Robert Gordon's College, Aberdeen, for my education, and guidance towards a philosophy of life.

Andrew Panton, Lincolnshire Aviation Heritage Centre, who supplied technical information regarding the Lancaster and crew.

There is no greater legacy than to bring the truth to those that are deceived.
For those that could lose the opportunity to be in the wonderful kingdom of God.

Pray for the Messiah to return;
Timothy M. Youngblood

Author/Steward of The Master's table

http://www.masters-table.org

Introduction

The subjects in the story occur at random – there is no sequence. They are buried in the cemetery or live in the area around it, and many can stand on their own as long as one knows the setting.

Several poems scattered throughout the prose later on do not have a connection to the text before or after. Their link is to the soldiers in chapter one. I have not put them between the early paragraphs because it would have broken up the flow of that part of the story.

Synopsis

An examination of the human condition based on a war cemetery, depicted by vignettes of members of the armed forces, civilians and flora and fauna, which explores the deeper truths in life, the horror and futility of war, and the beauty of life and peace. An overview of humanity that encompasses war, pacifism, anti-Semitism, genocide, human rights, religion, science, nuclear weapons, environment, equality, emotions, feelings and family.

Chapter 1

Serried ranks of virginal white stone, your heads held high as you did in battle, a vanguard at the gateway to the battleground; a white cross, a sentinel over the lake and the nearby sea marches on before, reflecting the memories of time. You, so innocent, your youth was taken away from you; your hopes and dreams extinguished like a candle. You are going nowhere now there is no rush to escape from the bullet and energy released with the blast of splintered steel.

You faced the enemy whose thoughts were the same; it was kill or be killed, with the strings being pulled by the men at the top of the chain of command. You were the puppets and faced death every day in your minds. The cross that you bore was heavy after killing a fellow human being; you saw his eyes follow yours as he crumpled to the ground. You hoped that it would be at a distance, and you would not see the agony on his face. Your sleep was the disturbed sleep of the damned; there was no peace for your soul by day or night. The demons of terror kept springing up, laughing at you as you tossed and turned, never allowing any rest; you questioned the meaning of life as another day dawned.

You prayed that another comrade would not fall, never to rise again, whom his loved ones would miss. You found friendship and support from those dead men's souls; relatives were far away from this cauldron of inhumanity. They ran with you, ate with you, and fought with you; some, mere boys whose schoolbags had barely left their shoulders. You did not want to get too close to those left alive so that your grief would be less if they died, but you had to have a friend to relate to otherwise you would have felt like a killing machine. You had to have faith in a fellow human being or else you would have gone mad – and how many of you did? You were sucked into a role that was abhorrent to you, and experienced terror and repulsion at the thought of killing; you were condemned if you did not shoot.

Others inured themselves to the killing: it was for country. But how often in the past had it been on behalf of country? You did not ask for that lunacy, you did not beg to go, the hierarchy forced you into battle. You hoped that you would never have to fire; you prayed that having done it once or twice it would come more easily and you would stand a chance of survival. You promised yourself that you would never enjoy it.

You had two choices: to stay put and risk a bullet or to climb over the top and risk a bullet; the overpowering fear was of being a coward. You went with the knowledge that in all likelihood you would at best be seriously injured, or worst killed. You knew that you would join your friends in that place where there is peace and tranquillity, and your souls could reunite.

You ran forward zigzagging with your compatriots; raked by gunfire you fell in your thousands amidst poppies in your first experience of battle. Your bodies lay in lines, limbs bent at awkward angles, some seeming to embrace when you fell on each other's chests.

Your commanders hoped you would overcome the enemy by force of numbers, and sent and received communications by paper messages from runners ordering you to attack. They were comfortable in their headquarters and did not go near the front line to see the slaughter and lack of advance.

A comrade received a shot in his chest but kept on running. He approached barbed wire, and to enable you to pass over, fell on it with his arms at right angles, his repose a cross. He lay there for a day while the battle continued – slipping in and out of consciousness – hoping the end would come; death would be a relief. The moon presided over the grisly scene; he saw it wax, he saw it wane. He saw his mother, sister and father cross the sun. The light went out, there was dark, a never-ending dark. He inspired, he exhaled, he expired; eternal peace, free from the barbarity of war.

A sergeant, who confronted an enemy, received a drill hole in his forehead and an exit wound of splintered bone and brain. He fell, clawing at the side of a trench before his bayonet entered the German's heart. The German's look of satisfaction turned to horror; blood poured along the floor. You became used to the stinking blood that covered your uniforms, which you might have to wear for days if the battle was fierce, and the rats welcomed it. His body lay until the end of the attack, an ever-present reminder to his comrades of their mortality. After a short time at the front line you became numbed to the ever-present thought that you could die. You sent reassuring letters of love to family about life in the trenches. You could not write about comrades who had died. Many of you thought that you would never see home again.

The battlefield was a scene of destruction and carnage – it was insane, that madness – human beings slaughtering each other. NOTE 1 Acrid choking fumes escaped from the sepia coloured earth when an explosion tossed a hand clasped in agony, and a fist clenched in rage across a massive shell crater.

Men lay separated from their amputated legs, faces racked with pain, their lifeblood haemorrhaging from their stumps into Mother Earth; a ragged arm still beckoned your colleagues to follow in attack. Soldiers protected from a blast by two right-angled bends in a trench scrambled to safety, trampling on dead friends. The enemy had found the range. Another shell landed. A brain from a detached skull scattered a mousse of porridge on the mud; one eye hung out on a nervous stalk from a head cut off by the slice of steel, the mouth set in rictus. A soldier's bowels spewed onto the ground from a gaping rent in his abdomen, the bloody mess of giant spaghetti squirming with nervous tension like a nest of vipers. A corporal's chest stove in, ribs flailing, pumped a geyser of blood into a pool over his collapsed lungs. A comrade, who sustained a direct hit by a shell, was present – then absent.

You reached the brow of an anonymous hill,
And saw the horrific scene.
A puff of smoke, a thump delayed,
And shells landing from their arcs.
They exploded at their sites,
Causing complete and utter destruction.

A EULOGY TO ABSENT FRIENDS

> A pockmarked moonscape,
> Added to each minute.
> A Dante's hell of incessant noise,
> Conflagration and mutilation,
> So far removed from home,
> And its quiet sleepy villages.

When the bombardment had finished you expected an attack. An officer looking through a periscope to prevent him being shot by a sniper saw the Germans surging forward, and ordered you to fire. Wave after wave of them poured across 'no man's land', and despite many being killed, there was always another to run into the breach. They swarmed onto your trenches, jumped over dead friends, and threw grenades and bombs. Blood cascaded down the chest of an officer whose face had been torn away by the grab of steel; brain seeped through the fissures between fragments of a skull crushed like an egg. A corporal blinded by a blast lay in a stream that ran along a trench, his uniform soaking up muddy water, making him shiver with pain and cold. The trench was defended with huge loss of life, and the Germans retreated.

After another exchange of shellfire you were ordered to attack, and had to climb over bodies waiting for transfer behind your lines. A soldier hit by the withering fire of a machine gun fell onto barbed wire, twitching when each bullet hit him. He bounced on the wire, his head lolled up and down twice, his body lay there for a few seconds, and then he slumped to his knees appearing to be praying for forgiveness. A private carried on for a few paces after his head was blown off, blood pumping out of his neck, drowning buttercups and clover; no four leaf ones were to be found. Your coats, sodden with water and plastered with mud, weighed twice as much again, and made you look like moving termite mounds. A horse, a line of bullet holes punched across its flank, pitched to its knees and catapulted a soldier, impaling him on a barbed wire support post. The horse whinnied, rolled onto its side, eyes staring and tongue hanging out, gave a plaintive cry, and died.

You tried to sleep, perchance to dream, about the nightmares of the day, of the last breaths of a friend as you cradled his head, and hopes that this war of attrition would have ended by the time the sun rose once again. You awoke in a sweat at the guilt you felt that a friend had died and not you. You were impotent to prevent it. The dark night of the soul followed inevitably after each battle, your spirits gathering before their journey to visit the newly deceased.

A spray of machine gun bullets felled an officer when he was climbing out of a trench to lead a charge; he exsanguinated in seconds, blood running down into his crumpled helmet. Sand from a bag trickled down his neck, fanning out, collecting under his uniform, and eventually with the weight his torso, fell forward. An aggregate of shrapnel, sand, uniform and shredded bodies formed on the walls of trenches.

A weary horse struggled through axle deep mud with a load of shells, and came to a halt, panting. It stood with a pitiful look, knowing it would not be able to go on any farther, hung its head dejectedly, and went down on its knees. Men jumped to coax the exhausted animal and push the cart, and the horse and its load moved forward. Worn out with the constant ordeal of serving men in war, it wished it was back home grazing in grassy fields where there was peace, no noise and smoke, and no smell of cordite and death.

Prometheus, a Titan, stole fire and gave it to you. It was used with deadly effect in a flamethrower, a stream of burning liquid shooting forward for many metres and engulfing anything in its path, causing horrific burns.

Shell craters full of a cloying quagmire formed by rain and granules of earth sucked you down. With no one to help, you disappeared inexorably into the mud; Mother Earth claimed another warrior by asphyxiation at the end of his short life. Some of you died with no apparent injuries, killed by blast concussion when a shell exploded 40 metres away. Exploding shells throwing earth, stones, and timber from their impact sites buried some of you.

The constant thudding and exploding of shells traumatised you and made you cover your ears, waiting for the next one to land, squeezed into a little dugout in the side of the trench where you slept. A piece of material hung over the entrance, gave you some privacy, but did not protect you from shrapnel. There was no life; life did not exist. The word had no meaning; death presided. The pockmarked terrain was dotted with skeletal trees set in mounds of earth and large pools of muddy water, a terrain that was foreign to man and machine – Apocalypse then. Along part of the front line a river separated you from your enemies. When silence fell, and the river ran smoothly, fish jumped, catching hovering insects – there were no fishermen.

The sun rose out of the shimmering sea and surveyed the sorry scene. It had watched the barbarity and brutality of war manufactured to its own design.

A man propped up against sand bags held a severed hand in his other – a harrowing sight. He thought he might lose it if he laid it down. He could not move without it; it could not be prised from his grip. He wiped blood out of his eyes and it passed before him. A pet dog and his master embraced each other, the master trying to comfort the dog in their final moments, his inner rage at those who started the war fading. Piles of unused shells lay in heaps beside a silent gun, the gun crew scattered around it, their limbs bent at abnormal angles.

Some of you fell, head first into trenches where body parts had lain. The rank tissue remains touched your faces when you landed, the malodorous smell staying with you, not even sweetened by all the perfumes of Arabia. With the breeze came the smell of coagulated blood; the odour alerted you to the passage of stretcher-bearers who reassembled the dead into their component parts before removing them on anything they could find to bear the weight, sometimes wheel barrows. They plodded along the maze of trenches, their boots sinking into the mud where duckboards ended, making them stagger. They passed soldiers sleeping, slumped against the sides of trenches, or sitting in mud where they had slipped in utter exhaustion, unable to stay awake despite the icy, soggy mess. Rats scuttled along, hoping for dropped morsels of food more suitable to eat than humans. They devoured rotting putrid flesh filleted off bones, and attacked soldiers, biting into their exposed flesh if they were unconscious or asleep.

In the distance, the inferno of burning buildings shone through the damp vapour casting a warm glow on the dark, subterranean pit that was your excuse for a home. The morning mist clinging to the ground wreathed and shrouded your bodies, enfolding you in its cold embrace of mortality while you waited clearance; casualties from the ongoing battle. The rising golden orb, no cross aloft, and the heat from the battle dispersed the lingering clammy fingers that enveloped you; it would return daily to creep over Mother Earth, a symbol of hope and life.

A code of honour existed, a truce was made, so that it was possible to remove the dead and injured from the battlefield with some dignity; it was not kept to respect the dignity of those left alive. Germans, isolated after an attack, and realising that they would not be able to fight their way back, surrendered, their wounded taken for treatment the same as their enemy; their wounds made them equals.

At Christmas, peace on Earth was made for a short time to celebrate the coming of the Saviour. You crossed 'no man's land' to greet each other with 'Happy Christmas' and sing 'Silent Night' while exchanging gifts, heartfelt by soldiers on both sides, but not by their superiors. You were friends, but enemies, driven by the wish for power of the leaders of countries who ordered their armed forces to war.

A copse stood on a devastated landscape, an island of green on a sea of brown. Beneath a tree, surrounded by lush grass, wild flowers and ferns, was an oblong mound of earth. At one end there was a wooden cross with a crucifix with Christ hanging from it, which had not been desecrated; it glinted in a shaft of sunlight that bathed the shallow grave. He viewed the horror of war once again and showed you mercy knowing you would atone for your sins. Some wild flowers that had been laid on the grave had withered, and there was the impression of two knees on the earth. A bird sang in a lull between the barrages.

At night, noise was the only guide for the enemy, and silence was essential. By the light of the moon you could see shadowy figures. Phosphorescent star shells illuminating the night sky magnified your terror, the explosive force's evolutionary history derived from the stars. Faceless apparitions ghosted into your apology for sleep: the ones that you killed at long range. Helmeted screaming banshees, wide eyed with dilated pupils, flared nostrils, and contorted faces reared up from the ground: the ones that you killed at short range. They were your companions in what was euphemistically called 'rest'. There was no rest for the wicked, which circumstances beyond your control had made you. Every friend lost floated before you by day and night, except when you were involved in battle. Forever imprinted in your minds, they had given their lives so that you might live another day; tormented with guilty thoughts you questioned why they should die, and you live.

You always hoped that the killing would be at long range; you squeezed the trigger, there was a bang, and someone in the distance flopped over like a bag of potatoes: at close quarters you had another face to fill your insomniac gyrations. You were close when you encountered him and took him unawares; he turned lifting his gun and you saw blind terror in his eyes when he faced death. You thought there was no possibility of him surrendering; your finger started to squeeze the trigger as he continued his turn; there was no thought other than self-preservation; there was no time for pity, self-recrimination, or turning the other cheek and offering the hand of friendship: any hesitation and you were dead. It was him or you: you had done it before. Spared to defend yourself on another day, you felt relief when he dropped. He would not have welcomed you as a long lost friend, and yet you were long lost friends of the human race. Your two souls floated free, enemies on Earth, on the same side in eternity, your dog tags and identities lost, but equals in the eyes of God; your bodies protected like children nestling in Mother Earth

> In the midst of conflagration,
> You surpassed with bravery,
> With an arm shake of defiance,
> You fought for your country.
>
> With a mind of fearless courage,
> And a spirit that was redeemed,
> You rose in resurrection,
> And let the future do what it deemed.
>
> In the throes of your renaissance,
> And exaltation at being free,
> When you turned yourself to loving,
> Your soul entered eternity.
>
> Joy came in an endless stream,
> As the darkness left the night,
> Sorrow with all its regalia,
> Was pushed away by the light.
>
> Happiness came in a flush of warmth,
> And an ushering out of grief,
> Now there would be no more fighting,
> And pointless loss of life.

On mornings, the gossamer dartboard of a spider's web, laden with dew, hung from your suspended helmets. The eight-legged aggressor ventured out to consume any captives ensnared in its trap, which it could feel along its trip wire. When the flaming ball reached its zenith, the heat baked you sheltering in your makeshift abodes. You waited for the next onslaught, slaking your thirst with water that was sometimes hot enough to have a bath – a bath – chance would be a fine thing. You knew it was good for morale and discipline not to appear dishevelled and unkempt, looking at your outwardly best when you felt at your inwardly worst, when you were going to kill another human being or be killed. It made no difference to him when dead. It made no difference to you. Comrades might say you died with military deportment and acting your best, and they would understand how you felt; the inner turmoil, anguish, and self-doubt. They would know that you were released from your torture.

> During war, should humanity pass judgment on a soldier if he kills an unarmed enemy, who has surrendered, in retaliation for the death of a friend? Only those who had experienced the emotional turbulence of their soul could do this. If an assailant killed a defenceless relation, and a weapon was to hand in any shape, how many could say in all honesty that they would turn the other cheek and forgive the attacker. In war, how much more strength is needed when friends are killed every day, and that was your raison d'etre. Could non-combatants understand when your emotional prop was lost repetitively in such a short

space of time? You got up, killed, ate, marched, snatched sleep with nightmares, killed and survived. Could you condemn a man for loss of control when no one could measure his feelings in this situation? He did not do it for enjoyment: he was not killing for gain. Did blind rage fire his gun? He killed because the person in his life to whom he related, his psychological support at that point in time, had died. Those of you who survived could not talk about what you had experienced; you could not put it into words – killing humans – seeing colleagues and civilians killed in such a horrific way. It was a visual experience and the associated emotions were indelibly imprinted in memory, rarely, if ever, to be discussed with comrades, never discussed after the war, and never forgotten.

On a bright summer day in 1944, humankind regressed: the forces of darkness descended on the defenceless French village of Omadour-sur-Glane. Six hundred and forty-two children, women and men were murdered by the SS, the men shot, and the women and children burned in the church; an atrocity beyond comprehension with no words in any language to describe it. If some of these men had been captured would the Allied forces have been able to restrain themselves, or relinquish their admission to heaven, killing them and joining their captives in hell? Would humankind have cared? Would their commanders have turned a blind eye, or would they have court-martialled them for contravening the Geneva Convention? There is a notice at the entrance to the martyr village that says

'Souviens-toi' (Remember). The village has been left as it was when it was destroyed; a visible memory of man's brutality.

A man sat petrified in a trench up to his ankles in icy water, his gun at his feet, and his coat stiff with the bitter cold. His frozen stare could penetrate steel, yet he saw nothing – visual information was blocked – his brain was not able to scan and process; he was virtually blind. He could not express how he felt or why he was there: he had no volition. His brain could not instruct his body to move, just as a rabbit is transfixed with terror in the headlights of a car. He could not defend himself or initiate aggressive acts, but instinctive survival reflexes persisted, driving him to escape from the noise: he shook violently; he had 'shell shock'. Some, cajoled into action, plodded pathetically and laboriously forward in no fit state to fight, adding nothing to the fray.

> Death was liberation from your sins of commission, but some in the past had paid for their sins of omission, for not facing up to kill, and being killed by someone on their own side. Those were the dark days in the not too distant past when there was no understanding of depth of feeling in humankind. Post Traumatic Stress was not a diagnosis that leapt eloquently to the lips, instead it croaked feebly in the throat like a hoarse bullfrog. Now there are armies to counsel the stressed; then armies took no counsel for the stressed. In some of you it manifested itself in a change of character that was unfamiliar, and not universally recognised at the time, but needing emotional support. In some of you it led to a

temporary shut down, unfortunately, in a few to lock down, and not able to do any meaningful work for the rest of your lives.

You march with your companions with the messages of love on your chests; no longer will you be beaten into subjugation by the volleys of metal threatening to kill you. You have given all: you can give no more. When will soldiers never have to make the ultimate sacrifice? When will there be friendship and lack of strife in humankind? You did not ask for much; you did not ask for immortality; you only asked for peace. You experienced despair every day in your quest for release from misery; you endured it at the beginning of the war; you suffered it at closure. It was hard to break the shackles of sadness and at the end there was no escape.

> Above this patch of foreign land,
> The clouds go scudding by,
> One more day in eternity,
> Your souls ask the reason why.

> Why man's depravity,
> Sometimes sinks so low.
> When will he start loving?
> And never have any foes?

> In this centrepiece of Hell,
> Stood the cesspit of immorality,
> And in your selfless sacrifice,
> Will our selfish love suffice?

> There will always be a special day,
> To remember your mortality,
> But when the next comes round,
> Will peace on Earth be reality?

Darkness descends; the black cloak of death stalks relentlessly across the parade ground, its fingers clinging remorselessly to all those souls adrift, signifying the folly and futility of war. A nightingale singing a lament interrupts the silence, and a deathly hush falls over the parade when homage is paid to you for your sacrifice in the fight for good over evil.

Your uniforms are now crisp at the edges, no longer are they crumpled and dirty. You lie in the arms of Mother Earth, which you did so often in the past. Then you waded through a decomposing morass of mud that impeded your advance on the enemy, and cut a huge swathe through the gently swaying grass and wild flowers of the countryside, turning it into a mire that oozed its way into your boots, which made your feet soggy and sore. It wet your uniforms, which stuck to you like a poultice, making you shiver uncontrollably from cold and fear. When there was water in the trenches you had to sleep standing – there was nowhere to lie. As a result, the circulation in your feet was compromised, often leading to Trench Foot. A layer of lice used to line your infrequently washed uniforms – they did not keep out the penetrating damp. If food was in short supply they complemented your rations – their bites caused Trench Fever. Could civilians imagine trying to sleep under those conditions night after night? You collapsed from physical exhaustion – there was no respite from mental fatigue.

Rain has washed the blood from your hands and the tears from your eyes, the sun has bleached the blood white in your wounds, the wind has dried it and gently eased off the superficial scars, but the deep scars will never heal – they are there forever – will man ever learn?

Now there are equal spaces in your togetherness with your friends and enemies, during battle there was chaos and separation. Here you lie buried with symmetry between your ranks, men of different creeds, colours and classes; how death is the self-levelling equaliser of humanity. The winds of time gently caress your proud upstanding memorials, eroding the messages when storms violently buffet you.

Rain splatters the ochre soil on your boots, but they remain stained when the fine weather returns because you are unable to polish them. In spring and summer, pilgrimages are made to your shrines to pay homage. You all pass muster in your uniforms of resplendent white; resurrected from Mother Earth they sparkle, reflecting you in all your glory. You will march into relative immortality.

As the Earth rotates, and the sun appears to move in an arc across the sky, the shadow of the cross scans some of your chests, tracing your destinies down through the centuries. The solar circle touches and microscopically weathers your epitaphs in its endless task of supplying energy to Earth. Your memorials are replaced so that we do not forget your sacrifice, and humanity will remember by ongoing conflicts in the world. Time moves on into summer and the shadows from your tombstones shorten, the threat of war diminishing for several months. On cloudless nights, the moon casts an eerie glow on your marbled features; at times its benevolent smile disappears when it forms a crescent trying to embrace your souls in its cool, calm embrace. War and Death, two of the Horsemen of the Apocalypse, inflicted visitations on you, and galloped off to ride through time, their black cloaks streaming behind them, and their evil laughter echoing down through the centuries; waiting to ride horseback once again on man's sins. Death will always ride through time, but will war, the antecedent of famine and disease, ever be dismounted?

On those still, hot, humid days,
With the dead weight of your packs,
You marched along at double time,
Sweat running down your backs.

In the fields of growing grass,
Stood coppices for protection,
They served as camouflage,
And hid the enemy's intention.

Through killing and through passion fields,
You fought and crawled along,
You gained no initial impression,
That it would go on for so long.

At the outset it seemed like
A great big comrades outing,
But soon after the dramatic start,
It was not over bar the shouting.

Scything waves of piercing bullets,
Cut you down in your prime.
So very few of your best friends,
Would live their due full time.

And time was of the essence,
In trying to end this war.
Instead, it ground on and on,
Both sides endured endless gore.

Your leaders made magnificent plans,
For conquering your foes.
They all went far awry,
Leaving you in the throes.

In the throes of violent battles,
You and your adversary.
For how many years from the start,
Would there be anniversaries.

In Flanders fields the poppies,
Bending in the breeze,
Make wave after wave of whispers,
Your torment they try to ease.

This pain is always borne,
By those who embrace your soul.
And they will carry it with them,
As they try to reach their goal.

Their goal is arms abolition,
And goodwill between mankind,
To unite the people of this Earth,
And make them of like mind.

Surrounded by your colleagues,
In the Earth's warm embrace,
You are safe in death,
By God's given grace. [1]

Chapter 2

Here lies an aviator; wings upon his chest, reaching for the sun, in adversity aspiring for the stars, whose plane lost its course when clouds covered them. NOTE 2 A cone of radar directed searchlights of many candlepower caught it, and streams of tracer forming red arcs lighting up the sky like a commemorative firework display found their course.

The navigator, a bright young lad, left university mid-course to serve his country in its struggle against evil. He knew that good would prevail and he would return to his studies, but only when his country had kept the enemy from invading. At home he had a sweetheart; at the end of a tour of duty – many never made it to the end – they enjoyed going out dancing with friends on Saturday nights. They did not talk about the horrific casualties among the bomber crews; they preferred to live for the moment. She plotted the course of planes approaching Britain across a large map of Britain and Western Europe, pushing blocks of wood with the height and the number of enemy aircraft on them; she might chart his return home.

He sat behind a curtain to allow him to use a light to work; a repeater gyro-magnetic compass, and his instrument panel showing air speed, altitude and other parameters needed for navigation were mounted on the fuselage above his chart table. He had to plot the plane's course using dead reckoning; there were no GPS with radio signals to guide it by waypoints over Germany. His astrodome gave 360 degree vision for celestial navigation, and on cloudless nights he could obtain repeated star fixes using a bubble sextant. He consulted a celestial almanac that he used to compute their path to near the target as the plane changed position relative to the stars. He could see the Milky Way, wonder about the Universe, and why, and what humankind was doing to itself on this pinhead in time.

Sometimes he saw the Northern Lights, the visible spectrum of light that gives us life, the sign that at night in part of the world the sun was still alive. If they passed through an electrical storm they sometimes experienced the St. Elmo's fire phenomenon when the aircraft became electrified. Huge light rings appeared round the propellers, and blue flames at the wing tips and guns. The sight of the blue-green jet of the engine exhausts licking over the leading edge of the wings reminded him of Chemistry classes and the burning of elements – what his plane was going to do. NOTE 3

He laid a course for the target: Karlsruhe, in the Ruhr valley, a town in the industrial heartland of Germany. A hundred miles from the target his view of the stars became obscured and the plane started to drift off course. He reported to the captain that they should abandon the attack. At the first blast he was thrown against the airframe and sustained a severe head injury; his charts, compasses, pencils and rulers burned in the flames.

The bombardier got married and his wife became pregnant, despite knowing the risk of death was considerable. His younger brother, not of the age to fight, but desperate to do so, was evacuated to the country with other children; some of the older ones were sent to work on farms. They usually travelled by train in school groups with their teachers – their labels with their name, and the name of their school on them tied to their coats. They carried parcels of clothes, girls a doll, and their gas masks round their shoulders in cardboard boxes. They were given a satchel of food to take to the family they would be staying with. Their parents were often not told the date of departure for security reasons. At the departure site, if they had been informed, mothers and fathers walked hand in hand to the station with their children, and exchanged tearful kisses when they said their goodbyes, not knowing when they might see each other again.

On the train, faces stared out of a compartment window with 'SMOKING' written on it. Young ones forlornly sucked their thumbs, older ones smiled, thinking it was going to be an adventure. They went on long journeys to places they had never heard of, in apprehension of what they might find at the other end. Some, who were sent to country houses had not been to the country before and were afraid of the farm animals, others were surprised to find fruit grew on trees. Most of them from the slums were surprised to find themselves staying in houses with inside toilets and carpets, the people who received them were surprised to find that they had not been 'potty trained', and had poor table manners; they slurped their soup and held their cutlery incorrectly. Children who lived in safe areas were not evacuated, carrying on studying at their local school, and taking exams. The schools had reinforced walls to withstand a blast, and tape was stuck across the windows to prevent large shards of glass being blown into the classroom.

His position was in the front cupola, which housed a gun, until the plane reached its target, when he moved to his bomb aiming equipment, taking over from the navigator for the final approach. He used an analogue computer to calculate the correct trajectory; from ground speed, wind direction and speed, and altitude, until the cross was over the target site and the bombs were released. If the target was obscured by cloud, pathfinder bombers lit the target with incendiary bombs. Over the target the bombers were packed closely together, and at different heights, with the risk of collision between aircraft, or dropping their bombs on each other.

When the navigator reported that they should abandon their attack, the pilot pulled the plane into a steep turn. The flight engineer pushed the throttles to maximum revolutions, the airframe shuddered, and the plane powered round, slicing through the sky. The pilot levelled out and ordered the jettisoning of the bomb load to ensure they would have enough fuel to get home, and to prevent the bomb load exploding if the bomb bay sustained a direct hit; the plane lurched upwards relieved of the weight. They hoped the bombs would land on open countryside; unfortunately, they fell on a town killing many innocent people in bed, and animals in fields. When the first shell hit the cockpit the bomb aimer received a mortal wound to his chest, exsanguinating in seconds, and blocking the forward escape hatch.

On the long flights, up to eight to ten hours, the pilot had the option to use an early form of autopilot named 'George' to fly the plane on its long journey across Europe; change of course was fed into it from the navigator's instructions. NOTE 4 It gave him a rest from thinking about holding the plane on its course and flying level before they reached Germany – he had enough to worry about when they flew near air defences and the target. During the flight, the incessant noise of the four Rolls-Royce engines deafened him: the soft glow of the instrument lights shone on his face.

His father was a devout Christian, who attended mass daily; he explained his construct of life to a friend whose lack of faith had never been challenged. Those who don't go to church think that people who do are pious; true Christians go to church because they know they are not perfect in their eyes. Only one person was perfect and He was tortured and brutally murdered; his sacrifice was so that we would be forgiven for being imperfect. What is important, what really matters is the contentedness of the soul, the inner peace of the spirit, holding to the truth in your heart that you always try to do the best you can, even though it may be wrong in the eyes of others who want to lead their own selfish way. We are all answerable to our own consciences and actions.

He was severely injured when shrapnel came through the Plexiglas cockpit, which opened like a flower in a gale, and slumped over the control column, blood running from his mouth and chest. The instrument panel was torn loose and crumpled, the glass on dials shattered, their bent hands fixed in their last position, control column linkages snapped, throttle levers buckled, and wiring looms torn off leaving wires flapping about in the hurricane. The cockpit was rewired, multiple short circuits sparking round it. The intercom was destroyed, oxygen pipes torn, hydraulics ruptured and cables leading to the control surfaces severed.

The flight engineer sat on his folding seat on the starboard side of the cockpit monitoring the dials that indicated engine performance, including oil pressure and temperature, and engine temperature. He adjusted pitch, flaps, trim, fuel mixture, and engaged the superchargers, setting the manifold boost pressure to maximum at take off, and altering it to maintain altitude during the flight. During take off, the pilot's hand was followed by his when the throttle levers were moved forward; he turned the locking nuts to hold them in position. He watched fuel levels in the tanks and adjusted the cross feed to maintain the plane's balance, altering the engine settings to try to conserve fuel to ensure the plane made it home with enough to spare. Both the pilot and the flight engineer could reach the throttle levers and the propeller speed controls, which were mounted in a central console.

Thirty minutes into the return journey, the oil pressure dropped and the engine temperature rose in the outer starboard engine, followed shortly by a failure of the reduction gearing, resulting in a drop in speed; the flight engineer feathered it. He was bending down facing to starboard at the time of the first explosion and missed the full blast, but sustained a deep laceration to his arm, which bled profusely; he staunched it by tying his flying scarf round it. His face was covered with small lacerations from shards of glass and he lost his vision in one eye. He managed to drag the pilot out of his seat, lay on him, pulled himself onto his seat and sat up; the gale pinned him to its back – a near impossible movement. He found the control column was jammed and fought to hold the plane as it descended through 20,000 feet, bitterly cold air blowing into the cockpit, freezing his face and hands, despite his gloves.

A shell hit an aileron and the oil feed system on the outer port engine, which caught fire; a plume of burning oil trailing from it. The flight engineer moved the throttle lever with his boot, shut the engine down, and feathered it. He pressed the fire extinguisher button but this had been damaged and did not work; with the loss of power the plane continued to descend at a greater rate. The inside port engine, which had received a peppering of shrapnel, overheated when ethylene glycol poured out of the cooling system. It started running rough, pistons and bearings ran hot, and it seized. With the loss of power from three of its engines it was doomed: he was trapped in the cockpit by flames behind him.

At the rear of the plane the rear gunner, 'tail end Charlie', aged eighteen, had kicked out a panel from his turret to increase his chances of seeing German night fighters. He constantly swivelled his guns to try to catch sight of any approaching, and fought one off on the outbound flight. The German planes were fitted with upward facing canons and could not be seen when attacking from below; the Lancaster was an easy target. If a German plane were spotted, the captain would send the Lancaster into a 'corkscrew', an evasive manoeuvre that involved diving and rolling the plane to left and right. At 22,000 feet, the air temperature could get as low as -40°C, and with no heating in his turret he had to put on layers of clothes; his oxygen mask froze to his face. He sat in a cramped space for eight hours; there was not enough room for him to fly with his parachute on his chest. He had to hang it on a mount in the fuselage, making escape from a stricken plane difficult. He was a joker, the live wire in the crew, and helped keep up their morale – and his own – necessary in his exposed position on the plane. His favourite phrase after briefings was 'nil bastardo carborundum'. NOTE 5

His brother, another joker, was a leading aircraftsman who loaded bombs. On big ones they would write graffiti – 'Best Wishes to Hitler'. His sister left town to work on a farm as a land girl, driving a tractor because the young men had gone to fight. She wore dungarees and a scarf around her head when harvesting crops, to prevent her hair being caught in the open turning machinery of the tractor and binder. When the crop had been bound into sheaves they propped them upright to dry, like a North American Indian tipi. NOTE 6 The farmer's wife used to bring tea and scones with butter and jam on them out to the fields; she enjoyed a good diet living on a farm. The battle in the air could be heard in the distance, and when a German pilot parachuted into a field in which she was working he was threatened with hayforks and taken prisoner.

Towards the rear of the plane there was a gaping hole, but the rear gunner's turret had escaped with minimal damage. Below it a fragment of steel had lodged in the turning mechanism; to escape he had to rotate it. Tortured, immobile steel groaned unheard, the motor moaned, and cogs ground while their teeth, which had been distorted out of true, tried to engage; the electro-hydraulic power unit burned out as it tried to overcome the block on the final drive. It was not possible to rotate the turret manually, and because his exit into the plane was turned away he could not reach his parachute.

The fire moved towards the tail of the plane; his intercom was burnt, he was on his own, and his screams could not be heard.

The mid-upper gunner's sister was a nurse in an industrial city that was bombed heavily, many casualties suffering severe injuries; his parents lived in London, near a tube station. When the siren went off before raids they took refuge with many others, some between the lines when the electric current had been turned off. There was camaraderie between them; they sang songs and supported each other, they were not going to surrender to Hitler – they would rather die. They would adjust their lives wherever possible, continuing 'business as usual' – Hitler underestimated the British tenacity and spirit.

Some had Anderson shelters in their back gardens where a family could 'sleep' in bunks until the raid was over. They protected against falling shrapnel and debris, but not a bomb falling close by. They kept a meagre supply of food that had to last a month; tea and blankets helped keep them warm on cold winter nights. They came to fear the 'on and off' sound of the twin-engine German bombers and the explosions of the approaching 'stick' of bombs.

Morrison shelters were rigid steel cages erected inside houses to protect the residents if the house came down on top of them. It was an offence to not keep a 'blackout': a black piece of material or paper, taped over windows to prevent light escaping, and make it difficult for German bombers to find their target. If a window was blown in, it exposed residents to the winter night. Unable to light fires, they wrapped up in layers of clothes. It was prohibited to have lamps on bicycles, and people who cycled to work struggled to find their way, especially if there was fog. Streetlights were turned off and traffic accidents were common because car headlights had to be shielded.

The first wave of bombers dropped incendiaries causing fires, lighting the way. The second wave bombs that killed and maimed, fractured gas and water mains, and reduced buildings to piles of rubble. After the raid had ended, when the 'all clear' siren sounded, they went to survey the damage; some found their loved ones dead. The next day unexploded bombs were cordoned off until defused, and residents within a set area asked to go to relatives or a rest centre, where they could sleep until accommodation was found for them. People struggled to work along streets full of debris. The emergency services searched for anyone buried. It was difficult for those who had lost everything to find the money for a funeral and buy black clothes; an allowance was given to them but provision of black clothes was not a priority, and they had to do without. [2]

The mid-upper gunner was forced down the plane by fire creeping along seeking nourishment, each finger becoming a hand, then an arm, greedily feeding it, never becoming full. He fell against a hot spar, sustaining a burn to his head and a deep laceration on his face, which poured blood. He stumbled on hot metal trying to make his way back to the rear gunner. His boots stuck to the floor making an acrid burning smell, which was immediately sucked out into the night sky. Another shell exploded near the plane and a piece of shrapnel hit him in the neck, slicing through a major artery.

The radio operator's station was to the rear of the navigator's table and forward of the front spar. In the centre section there was a 'rest bed' – a misnomer, which could be used if one of the crew were injured. A container at the rear of the plane was used for a toilet.

He had a small table with his radio, pads and pencils and a small window, but this was covered at night by a curtain to maintain a blackout. Bombers tried to confuse German radar by dropping strips of aluminium called 'window' or 'chaff'. An eighth crew member on one squadron used a microphone placed behind an inner engine to record the deafening engine noise, and transmit it on German ground-to-air radio frequencies – an early form of ECM (electronic countermeasures) – making it impossible for night fighters to speak to their controllers. Pathfinder planes that lit the target with incendiary bombs carried a radio operator who could speak German to intercept radio communications between German planes and the ground. They could tune in to the Luftwaffe night fighters and give false and misleading instructions. .

His father was a bomb disposal expert who defused unexploded German bombs – a special type of bravery was needed for performing this task when your deliverance sat in front of you. His mother worked long shifts, seven nights or days, in a factory building Lancaster bombers; she was proud to help the war effort, and only too willing to work longer hours. She received an hour's instruction on a milling machine, mastering it as quickly as a man. Heavy lifting was done using a hoist – she would fight to the end rather than let Britain be invaded. Her hands became rough and fissured like a labourer's with washing and constant contact with swarf and oil. NOTE 7

The blast threw him to the floor, his valves and dials shattered, no longer able to communicate. His face and arms peeled, exposing burned, red, raw tissue, which changed to black when it became charred; the smell of burning flesh did not linger. A slice of shrapnel scythed through an arm and leg, and spurts of blood escaped from his wounds onto the glass, which reflected the flames. He rolled over and the glass cracked and crackled.

The flight engineer climbed out of the damaged cockpit escape hatch with difficulty and was whipped away by the wind. But his parachute was damaged and the shrouds snagged on release. It only partially opened, and he plummeted to earth. The canopy enshrouded him as he lay at peace on the ground, no more to go where man boldly dared to go, his endless battle against the gravitational forces at last at an end. Mother Earth had gathered another son to her breast at the end of his quest for survival.

German bombers flew to destroy our industry, and the means of defending us: RAF fighters defended our country from them. The brave men of Bomber Command flew through the night sky, across the overworld, to destroy the industry that made their machines of war; come the morning they were born again with the rising sun – many passed into the afterlife. The strategy of Bomber Command was considered controversial later in the war because of the blanket bombing of German cities, and the death of hundreds of thousands of civilians. The role of the airmen was not recognised because there did not seem to be any positive benefit for the country. Without them, the war might have lasted longer and many more people would have been killed. To the shame of the nation their sacrifice has only just been recognised, and a memorial built of a crew gathered in reunion. NOTE 8

Some of you march beneath the shadow of a gnarled oak tree with its expression of tired resignation at man's futility; many were used to build ships for marine battles centuries ago. The ancient tree could not defend itself, and bled for a long time from a wound where a branch had been blasted away. Its lifeblood oozed in a trickle, hardening to form a thick, hard, translucent skin over the wound: at least it survived.

A family of squirrels, who had lived in the old tree for many generations, banished themselves when the laying waste started. Their descendants carried some of the oak's fallen children a short distance away from the parade, storing them for food over winter; some were dropped and will turn into saplings to continue the family tree, growing and branching with time. The squirrels respect the well-tended oblongs of Mother Earth on which you march. They look about warily, wending their undulating, staccato, tail-whipping way across the grass that your feet have never touched.

In front of the headstones of a sixteen-year-old lad who lied about his age, and a fifty-year old-man who wanted to join his relatives in combat, a colony of ants fight their own battles to prevent invasion by neighbours; an interminable conflict spanning millions of years now played out before you, a reminder that even in the insect world there is no peace.

A Peace Lily, planted since Armageddon, stands to attention, and from its vantage point in a nearby garden unfurls a white banner from around a gun-cleaning rod; its sign of truce. NOTE 9 Its sisters lying on the surface of a nearby pond had been present at the demolition, felt the heat, but the surrounding water saved them from the inferno.

A flight of ducks in V echelon passes over the cemetery at low altitude proclaiming victory for good over evil. All the birds, except the bird at the front, fly in the up-wash from the wing tip vortices of a bird in front, which helps to reduce drag, and thus flight fatigue. They rotate the lead position, the lead bird dropping a few feet and then falling back to the rear of the formation. Their leader looks for the nearby lake to land on, the curtains of the day drawing over the sun by which they are navigating. They have landed for millennia, by night to obtain a star fix, and by day to recalibrate their magnetic navigation systems to magnetic north by a pathway into their brains initiated by the sun. NOTE 10 They forage for food to assimilate into energy for the onward flight, food that is dependent on photosynthesis from the self-same sun, and a flight that is driven by evolution to enable them to survive. Then there was no possibility of landing safely with explosions and small craft crossing the lake. Now, on high, larks sing your praises in the heavens. Then they scolded you angrily in a statement of outrage, intruders encroaching on the territory where their nests lay.

The police carried out their usual duties catching intruders and burglars, but also profiteers, black market traders and looters (not just a twenty-first century occurrence). They assisted the Civil Defence workers during and after air raids, responding to sirens, assisting the fire brigade to put out fires, and checking ID cards. They monitored foreigners and aliens in case they were saboteurs or spies, and issued gas masks, visiting schools to undertake gas drills. Everyone carried ID cards and metal discs around their necks, including children, with their ID number, name and address, and changes of addresses: bombing destroyed homes. They were required in case families got separated from each other, or if people were killed or injured. Slogans were created warning against secret talk, and posters put up, one showing a caricature of Hitler sitting on a bus seat behind two people with the caption: 'CARELESS TALK COSTS LIVES'.

A bird of prey hovers above the parade, the sun reflecting off its steely eyes, its talons and hooked beak ready to tear the heart out of anything that moves. Its high-resolution vision seeks any variation in light waves, which enables it to see small prey on the ground. It twists its tail, banks, wheels, and adjusts the angle of wing trim to compensate for the loss of a feather. It manoeuvres to get the sun to its back, ensuring its victim cannot see the attack coming out of the sky, and intuitively calculates the angle of deflection in its power dive.

You had experienced an attack from a bird of prey, a phoenix that had risen from the ashes of Mother Earth in a foundry that was as hot as hell, spitting fire in an incandescent arc of light, which pulverized the earth around the graves that you had dug for yourselves. Lumps of hot metal flew over your heads embedding themselves in trees, obliterating wild flowers when the blast of hot gas hit them. You were deafened, and sods of earth and boulders rained down on your heads as you cowered in submission to this God of Death on whose altar many ritual sacrifices had been made; your blood running in streams and soaking into Mother Earth. Men who raised this god's idol long ago are still genuflecting in submission to it.

Chapter 3

Here lies a submariner, a ship shape sea dog anchored to Mother Earth by a periscope of white.

His boat shadowed an enemy ship using a search periscope, and after taking a 360 degree search, and seeing no warships, the captain ordered 'down periscope'; the attack one was raised to attain target acquisition from bearing, speed and range. The range was calculated using an enemy ship's recognition chart, which gave the height from the sea to the top of the ship's mast when an image of the target was superimposed over the actual image of the ship. The angle from the top of the enemy ship's mast to the submarine's periscope was measured using a split prism stadimeter. He shouted the measurements adding 'mark', and 'down periscope'; the information was fed into a TDC (Torpedo Data Computer), and a trigonometric calculation gave the range. The calculations were repeated several times over 10 minutes. The firing solution was given by the TDC. The gyrocompasses on four torpedoes were set, and they were launched. The submarine crash-dived to run silent and deep; the running time of the torpedoes was counted down second by second.

An enemy seahorse appeared from the other side of the convoy, heeling and lancing forward, propelled by many unbridled horses, and packed with immense destructive power; on board the Lutine bell tolled once. NOTE 11 The ballast tanks were flooded; the hydroplanes inclined down; the clinometer showed the maximum angle of descent, every second decreasing the chance of being detected. Its dive might take it below a thermocline, the stepwise gradients in ocean temperature that initiate and drive the convection currents necessary for the health of the ocean environment, in the same way that clouds and wind are necessary for the health of the land; an interface of two temperatures offered the chance of confusing the probing sonar waves emitted by the ship above; there was no hope of merging with the seabed below before the hull was crushed by the pressure and imploded. NOTE 12

The boat plunged down, ever down, into the domain of the denizens of the dingy deep, Proteus winding his giant coils around it. Valves were tightened to stop high-pressure water leaking through gaskets and seals. It made a zigzag course trying to shake off the sound waves from above; it was caught between the searching Scylla and the crushing Charybdis.

His craft was detected by the waves and the tone changed, pinging like a monotonous underwater orchestra – a harbinger of death. A hedgehog was fired bristling with menace, and a cylinder of destruction tolled the death knell on the casing; it exploded, shock waves bending the submarine like a ruler and ripping it open. Fuses blew and men were thrown into darkness until the emergency lights came on. The forward escape hatch was distorted.

The captain ordered full reverse and the helmsman rammed the gear lever home; full torque available instantaneously at zero revolutions from the electric engines.

The twin valve trains of push rods and rockers to outlet and inlet valves went up and down alternately like frantic 'nodding donkeys'; all undamaged ballast tanks were blown but the submarine continued its plunge into the abyss prow down; the depth gauge stopped rotating indicating the submarine was below its rated limit. NOTE 13

In the engine room water poured in, rivets popped, bolts blew, and distorted pressure plates groaned under the compression forces, the pressure exceeding the maximum they were designed to take; the crew hammered wedges into cracks, but it was futile. The Chief Engineer was blinded when a jet of hot oil from a fractured oil feed pipe shot into his face as he tried to coax maximum revolutions out of his dying engines; he fell against his baby. The engines' lifeblood spewed out onto the grating making a slippery carpet. Water and high-pressure air leaked through glands and joints; the submarine was caught in the jaws of a remorseless destiny.

The pumps were unable to keep up with the influx of bitterly cold water, which poured in, rising above the grating, and around the crew's feet. They grabbed at their life saving equipment, which was hanging on hooks, to try to prevent them falling over. But with the increasing angle of descent they slid down the wet metal deck banging into metal protrusions, which ripped their skin off, and gouged chunks of muscle.

Props were used to support torn flanges to stem seawater pouring in, and dowels were hammered into fractured pipes. Gaskets leaked, engine-cooling pipes fractured, and the exhaust flap was damaged. A member of the crew fell over, striking his head on a ballast tank valve, sustaining a deep laceration, and a sailor, who was trying to tighten a valve, was struck on the head by a flying bolt. Tortured bearings ran dry, smoke from burning oil filled the engine compartment; overheated armatures, coupled in parallel for maximum speed, emitted the smell of electricity, and water poured into the battery area releasing poisonous chlorine gas.

For a time the speed of descent slowed, but it accelerated when the engines lost power. In the aft torpedo room, a torpedo, torn from its rack by a blast, crushed a sailor's legs when he was struggling towards an escape hatch. A stream of hot water from a fractured pipe stripped the skin from a sailor's face; he fell to the floor in agony. The captain was thrown against the back of a sailor, who was pulling back on the hydroplanes, which were jammed in the down position. In the galley, cooking equipment fell, clattering towards the bow of the submarine; an oily scum followed them on their passage. The cook was flung against a sharp edge fracturing his arm. A vegetable and fruit cocktail of apples, cabbage and onions, followed by a string of sausages swilled down the floor; men tried to keep themselves erect by holding onto legs of pork hanging from hooks, which slapped their faces – the submarine hit the bottom.

Icy water rose inexorably to the crew's knees, the cold sweat of fear running in rivulets from their faces, mixing with sea salt. They banged on closed watertight doors to assess whether there was water on the other side, and if they could open them safely. A man, who was on the same side of a bulkhead as the ingress of water, had one of his hands crushed when the watertight door was shut; any delay to allow him to get through might have meant that the door could not close due to the build up of water in the next compartment. The sea rose towards their knees, their chests, and their chins. They pressed their faces against the air space in the roof of the compartment; they choked, they drowned, and they floated in their watery burial chamber. One man held onto the periscope housing and pulled himself out of the water, hoping in vain that he might see the sky again.

The navigator was in a compartment in which there were two metres of sea. The watertight doors on either side had been shut in time, but there was no lighting; he and two other men had access to an escape chamber. He fumbled his way across the black tomb, found the ladder to the inner escape hatch, and spun the wheel: it opened easily. He climbed into the chamber dressed in his life jacket and breathing equipment, which he had managed to find before the lights went out, and shut the hatch. He let in seawater through a valve, and it rose filling the chamber. When it was full, and the water pressure equalized on both sides, he struggled to open the outer hatch, which eventually freed. He kicked himself out of the submarine and inflated his buoyancy jacket, which lifted him towards the surface: he made a miraculous escape at that depth.

After a week, a school of dolphins came upon him; with their inscrutable smiles and sparkling eyes they chattered amongst themselves, teaching each other new noises. In formation, they arced out of the sea, and with a flick of their tails could spin through 1080 degrees. Synchronous and co-ordinated by communication between them, they could manoeuvre away from danger in seconds. Their geometric symmetry and strength in numbers was a deterrent to intruding predators breaking up the integrated school, which was maintained by tenuous yet binding electro-acoustic forces passing between them, necessary for their defence against being attacked on a one-to-one basis, and disruptively distorted by nets. They sensed the sound waves from the navigator's raft slapping in the water, and using echolocation, came to investigate. NOTE 14 They tried to communicate by touching him affectionately, but he had lapsed into unconsciousness and did not respond.

They knew from experience, because their actions and communications were pleasing they were safe from humans at this time in history – even when the humans sailed in powered craft. They would swim in front, their dorsal fins scything through the emerald sea leaving a phosphorescent steam of bubbles, which were divided by and merged with the bow wave from a ship, directing it to follow, and slowing to let it catch up. They did not know that in years to come low frequency sound waves from sonar might kill them, or the pod might drown in a mesh of netting, and fellow mammal relations would be hunted almost to extinction, killed by a harpoon in their backs.

An albatross – the eternal ocean wanderer, with its wing span of immense dimension and narrowness through evolution – cruised gracefully out of the ethereal stratum, searching for the souls of shipwrecked mariners, gliding into the wind at an angle towards the sea's surface to gain momentum, then altering the setting of the leading edge of its wings to attain lift and gain height.

The bird saw a boat, Red Cross on its deck, the crew no cross in penance about their necks. From its elevated position across the deep divide it spied the sailor, and led the boat towards the dolphins, drawing the attention of the rescuers to his plight. Alas, it was too late, for though there was 'water, water everywhere nor any drop to drink', dehydration killed him. He escaped from the raptures of the jet-black deep, only to succumb to the drought of the azure shallows. NOTE 15 NOTE 16 NOTE 17

> Faith doesn't ask why,
> It speaks not from the mind,
> It always believes,
> Rescuers will find.
>
> Hope aspires,
> It looks for a sign,
> It never denies,
> Until the end of time.
>
> Help may not call twice,
> It can come all at once,
> Or beckon from a distance,
> Without a second chance.

A bird pecks at worms that squirm in the newly turned soil in front of his grave, flicking it onto his feet. His father, who was 40, could not join the armed forces but signed up for the Home Guard, or Local Defence Volunteer. Formed when there was a risk that Hitler might invade Britain, they became known as 'Dad's Army'. Most of them had full time jobs and had to train in the evening; the public donated rifles, pistols and shotguns. As well as preparing to fight off an invasion, they guarded buildings that had been bombed to prevent looting, helped clear bomb damage, rescued people trapped after an air raid, guarded factories, captured German aircrew who had been shot down, and set up road blocks to check people's ID cards.

The Admiralty requisitioned trawlers into the naval service leaving a depleted fishing fleet. Most trawlers and trawlermen joined the Royal Naval Patrol Service, the ships serving as minesweepers; there was a heavy loss when carrying out this task. They came under fire from planes and U-boats on the surface and were fitted with guns. They helped in the evacuation of Dunkirk and rescued crews from sinking ships, as well as from downed British and enemy aircraft. Fish catches dropped dramatically during the war, and even though there was no rationing, the price went up making it too expensive for most of the population.

In the South Atlantic where submarines used to prowl in packs, dolphins, albatrosses and turtles are enmeshed in fishing nets and plastic bags made from the breakdown products of oil, which drift out to sea from the waterways that are used to irrigate banana plantations. The bags are used to cover the bananas, to ripen, and protect them from insects. Insecticide, which is toxic to humans, is sprayed inside the bags to reduce the amount needed, avoiding the widespread deposition of it by planes.
NOTE 18

A kingfisher – King of fishers, teller of tales, narrator of legends, master of his craft, bedecked in iridescent cobalt blue and orange, and endowed with infinite patience – perches on a branch at the side of the lake during a period of halcyon weather. NOTE 19 He has the ability to polarize light, reducing the reflection of it off water, and intuitively calculates the error for the angle of refraction of it through water; his knowledge born of experience gained by trial and error in his aim and flight. His queen and equal in their 'raison d'etre' of bringing up their young perches on a branch half a league beyond. NOTE 20

He told many a tale of the dwindling supply of fish in the lake, about the big ones that escaped, gone in a flash like quicksilver, too fast for his lightning strike. NOTE 21 He would emerge from his dive without a fish, droplets pouring off his waterproof plumage, and dripping off his beak.

Men fished the lake in their motorised craft, and oil from their engines poured on the water troubled him, his ability to fish sorely tried. NOTE 22 The shimmering iridescence of the essence of life, the light of life split into its spectrum of component colours to be eventually degraded by ultra-violet light, the distillate of the long-buried bodies of sea life, the volatile vapours trying to emulate the ephemeral beauty of them suspended in a bioluminescent haze in the sea, blocked his view, poisoned the fish, and prevented a pass through water without damaging his feathers. He gave many a discourse; how the supply of fish was once bountiful, when men in wind powered boats fished on a small scale, sharing the lake with fish catching birds.

He dreamed of long gone balmy, quiet days, when the caress of a zephyr flowed across the lake and life was peaceful; when fish rose and jumped near the shore, and there was no wake from a powered boat lashing the shore line, eroding away soil around tree roots, loosening and washing away reeds, and disturbing birds nesting; when there was no thump in the distance followed by a noise building to a hissing crescendo, a huge fountain of water erupting in the lake that made him take to flight, King of fishers though he was.

An overcast sky,
A suggestion of rain,
Who can assuage,
The endless pain.

For pain continues
In those you love,
And your spirits grieve on
In the heavens above.

The ascent of your soul
To this elevated state
In the memory
Of those who love you,
Is due to selfless actions
Throughout your life,
And for your country
The ultimate sacrifice.

CHAPTER 4

A woman, bereft, kneels in front of her son's grave arranging wild flowers. Unwelcome sadness, dejection and despondency have visited so many of your loved ones. Some have a site they can go to grieve, have a feeling of being at one with you; some have no site and feel the perpetual need to search for one, knowing you are not at rest in a place they can identify with. NOTE 23

A breath of cool air blows through the still atmosphere, shaking leaves; it sends a shiver down your backs, and makes flowers nod their heads in obeisance to an equal power. An ethereal, willowy woman with an enigmatic look enters the cemetery. The sun comes out from behind a cloud, shining in an endless, beckoning stream across the parade. The wind abates until there is absolute silence.

She drifts across the shimmering water, at peace with herself if not with the world, her destiny preordained on the whispers of the night to be forever attracted towards the negative forces of darkness, and to heal suffering and pain. She passes through your ranks; her head slightly bowed, a luminous passion in her demurely downcast eyes, her resolute resonance making her the epitome of empathy. She gently touches some of you on your march into eternity, bringing hope in her understanding of unhappiness.

J. N. SLATER

In her dreams she had lived
These moments many times before,
Fought these battles after many a war,
Hoped for peace and no more ugly scars,
Her faith and grace meaning there were no bars,
To helping those in pain both near and far.

Approaching the mother, who was inconsolable in her grief, she got down on her knees, and looking into her eyes, saw it all in that one moment in time. No words were uttered. In a silence that spoke louder than words she lit a flame in the mother's mind, lighting the way down the otherwise lonely path of hopelessness.

They touched, and there was a transfer of positive energy; the mother felt the ultimate truth in life, the truth that transcends all other channels of communication, the sustaining force of humanity, for although time moves on, true love out of sadness never dies. The mother ascended to the domain of the spirit on the wings of a love that asked no questions but gave all the answers, knowing no boundaries or prejudices, where souls congregated to sing your praises, and where she heard this epitaph.

You have not left,
You have merely stepped
Aside into your shadow,
Very much alive and
Never to be forgotten.
Your souls heard and remembered,
Living on in the minds of those
Who love you.

When she returned, the younger woman had departed to recharge the depleted energy of her soul from other like-minded ones, or those who would listen to her tales of horror – for no one can standalone.

Some of us, who carry a light load, cross the road to pass others who carry a heavy load, have fallen by the wayside and are in distress, needing help to move on. Some of us stop and give assistance from the depths of our hearts, draining ourselves and ceasing to function, needing help from others to recover our resilience. Some of us remain broken down, unable to be repaired, incapable of moving on despite acts of altruism.

The majority of women went out to work as civilians during WWII but those who did not worked at home cooking, cleaning, and ironing to support key workers. Many had to work in, and outside the home to earn money to support their family; a punishing workload, a load they never complained about. At the end of their long shifts they came home worn out, did their own work at home, and fell into bed exhausted. A stove heated by rationed wood or coal was used for cooking and heating the living room. Washing was boiled in the kitchen in a tub with a fire beneath it. They baked using dried milk and eggs, making cakes and wholemeal bread, which the family ate with a smear of butter and jam if they had not used their ration for the week. If they had finished their work, and were not involved in work outside the house, they would share a cup of tea with friends, talk about their worries for their men, exchange recipes, and get ideas to make food more tasteful. In the evening they would listen to the radio. The broadcasts were interrupted by German propaganda to try to undermine their morale. Special messages were sent giving information to British Secret

Agents. When the accumulator (a battery that had to be recharged at a radio shop) ran out of electricity, families retired to bed. In winter, people put house bricks in the oven to warm them, then took them to bed wrapped in a towel. During the night, frost formed on the inside of windows, and it was possible to write your name; there was no central heating, you had a bath in a cold bathroom or a galvanised zinc bathtub if you were not so well off. Water was heated on the stove.

Churches continued to be used for marriages and worship. Communities carried on much as usual with people going out to the cinema, dancing, and the pub (even women) in areas where there was bombing. The lights, music, and the company let them forget the misery, austerity and danger of war. Single ladies, ever resourceful, washed their legs in a solution of fine sand and water or diluted gravy salt to give the impression of wearing stockings, and put on leg make-up using eyebrow pencils to give the appearance of a seam. If there was a US Air Force base nearby, they would hang about outside in the hope of getting nylons and cigarettes passed to them through the perimeter fence. Invited to dances, they got to know the airmen, some getting married and going back to the USA at the end of the war – some of the airmen were shot down – their wives were pregnant. [3]

Despite the threat, and because everyone was fighting for the same cause, the morale of the nation was high. Some reported, when they were older and had not lost loved ones, that it was the best time of their lives – they lived for the moment – whatever would be would be.

> A bird perched in a tree that had a branch blown off, scratches its head in amazement at the parade.

She had laid her eggs and was going to hatch them, but the noise of battle had driven her away leaving them to go cold. The clamour, made by humans, made her take flight because she associated it with destruction. She collects with her friends at dawn and dusk making a considerable fanfare, welcoming the end of the fray, thankful for another day and the transition into peace and beauty

Here, at rest, lies one of you awarded a cross posthumously for valour, wearing it gouged on your heart for all time; you gave your life so that others would live another day. You gave covering fire for comrades when you were hiding in a church and came under attack; they escaped, but a shell came through the roof bringing it down. You died beneath a cross of roof beams transfixed by a nail, a bloody hole in your side and a look of peace on your face, knowing you had saved the others if only for a short time. Motes of dust danced religiously on a shaft of sunlight shining on your head through a hole in a wall, transfiguring you. Your friends looked on in remembrance, desolate at their loss, silently giving thanks. A circle of metal jammed against your head, although rusty, shone brightly in the sun.

> On hot and torrid days,
> When marching in the sun,
> Rifles raked, one arm straight,
> In rhythm with the beat.
> Thoughts of daring and of courage,
> At carrying out a feat,
> Now there is sadness and sorrow,
> Laid in remembrance at your feet.

A rabbit, bob-tailed, nose twitching, sits near the perimeter of the parade, nervously scanning the horizon for human intruders on her land through discharging slit eyes. She is able to fight the ravages of Myxomatosis, having developed partial immunity and genetic resistance. NOTE 24

She peers at the ranks of guards inside the wire mesh fence. The commandant, who presides over the ceremony, is dressed in a white uniform, his short arms sticking out at right angles: he is reverent, silent and straight faced. The rabbit had never seen him move, but thought that if she escaped into the compound he might do so. The lush grass looked inviting, but it was extremely short. However, it was always quiet, and there was no movement when she came out to feed in the field in the evening. On nights, when a full moon illuminated the way for her to set up a run from her warren to the parade, your tombstones receded into the distance showing perspective.

No information passed down through the generations concerning the noise made by the humans that killed her family and friends when they ran for their lives to their warrens; she had to learn through experience. She did not understand these silent, immobile guards, who were so different from the humans of whom she had experience. She knew that the sight of a human being approaching meant she had to hide because they were so unpredictable.

A snake slithers silently through swaying grass seeking small mammals to devour and savour. A lieutenant disturbed one sleeping under the bark of a fallen tree when he stealthily crawled towards an enemy gun emplacement. He separated long stalked grass and crushed wild flowers, disturbing insects and crickets chirping in the midday sun. When the breeze dropped, and the grass stopped moving, he lay motionless until it picked up again; five soldiers followed him. He came upon a ditch and slipped into it, moving towards the rear of the emplacement. When he was near, he heard the Germans talking casually and having a cigarette, unaware of his approach. A lookout scanned the horizon in front of the position, and seeing nothing, turned back to carry on talking. The lieutenant pulled the pin out of a grenade and tossed it but it hit the wall of the position, and bounced back wounding him. His comrades carried him back to the front line, zigzagging through scrub to try to avoid enemy fire. The injury caused massive bleeding and he died in a comrade's arms.

A deer – doe-eyed, flicking her tail, munching young saplings, pricks up her ears, turns, and sniffs the air inquisitively. When the breeze veers round to drift from the direction of the distant parade she can smell the scent of humans. During the war she smelled burning flesh, wood, metal and material across many miles of countryside when she retreated up a mountain to her hideaway.

She had often seen men with long sticks making a noise that terrified her, and friends fall down, never to move again, carried away unceremoniously hog-tied to a stick. She had watched the ceremonies in the enclosure where succulent saplings grew, which she could not reach because of the fence; her food supply was limited by human activity. People came and went, many with sticks they used to support themselves by pushing them into the ground when they walked.

During the war, fresh food was in short supply. School playing fields and parks were dug over to grow vegetables, and older adults cultivated allotments. 'A Dig for the Nation' poster appeared in public places. Bikes, or horse and cart, delivered milk, meat and groceries. Every part pf an animal was eaten – head, brain, stomach and pig's trotters; people were hungry – there was no alternative – obesity was almost unknown – they barely had enough to eat.

Chapter 5

Autumn prevails; the days close in; the nights lengthen.

> In dark you stand on an oblong of ground,
> A galaxy of stars in your eyes.
> Your souls drift free in perpetuity,
> To be blown about like dead leaves,
> On the mournful wind of the night.

The west wind lowers itself humbly onto its knees on its voyage in search of lowliness, soughing through the hallowed portals of the cemetery, and circling on its anti-clockwise way. Your souls have difficulty staying in touch with you. Leaves are blown through your ranks kissing your faces, pressing against the message from your loved ones, until a vortex frees them to dance their weary way across the parade ground to their maker, to the soundless tune from the band. NOTE 25

When the mists of time flow off the lake making a sea that engulfs the parade, your dignified heads rise above the hushed marching. The message from your loved ones is temporarily hidden but never lost; it always shines forth from your hearts emerging from the mists as permanent as before – no vapours can eradicate this loving paean to your soul. In battle you experienced a vapour of malevolent evil rolling over your heads, which caused internal and external bleeding, and damage to your bronchial tubes and lungs, resulting in death. Nerve gas was developed by Germany during World War I but it was never used. It is now being utilised with devastating effect, causing a horrific death.

Two ravens cloaked in black, undertakers of the animal world, peck at each other, bickering and squabbling over arrangements for Commemoration Day. One flies off to offer condolences, respectfully wiping its beak before tapping on one of your graves and straightening a cross with a poppy on it. It blows through the bristles outside its nostrils, distressed at the number of ceremonies it had had to undertake, carrying souls into the afterlife. They gather making unprofessional, raucous calls of anger, and then fall silent in veneration of you.

Heavily built with strong legs and a large beak; one picks up a large twig that has fallen on the soil in front of you and flies to its nest to continue building the ramshackle structure. It stole food from other birds, its advanced brain giving it the ability to remember where it was hidden, and how to locate it. It glanced askance at a crow, a lower ranking member of the family, hiding some food. Before flying away it lined up a headstone and a telegraph pole using its accurate spatial memory to get a bearing on the cache, and returned later to steal it for his young and mate. NOTE 26

One flies to a nearby scarecrow, gives it a look of utter disdain at its ability to scare, and picks some food that it had hidden out of the mouth of its death mask face; it buries it with reverence and kindness in its own secret place, and joins the unkindness. In sombre mood they progress in line with measured gait, hopping, staggering, sidling with eyes deviated towards the headstones. A chill wind blows round the gravestones ruffling the birds' feathers; the cortege processes at funereal pace towards the cross, and mimicking a human voice they vocalise 'ess u'. [4]

A cock pheasant struts sedately in solitude in the dawn light, his ceremonial plumage highlighted by the rising sun. He pauses pensively, wings behind his back, surveying the white rows of the parade. NOTE 27 At this time of day there is a deathly, palpable silence, until the members of his species start calling; no other sounds carry on the air, and he knows he is safe to be the in open.

He has to cross over land by air to find food, and risks being shot down. Many compatriots had gone down when they flew across the moors from their feeding place after their last supper, hit by salvos of lead flying up from hides, despite evasive manoeuvres. He had sustained some minor injuries in his battles with fellow males for territory; this was nature, it preserved the strongest of the species. He displays in front of females during courtship, and shows his dominance and aggression towards other males in defending his territory around the cemetery by enlarging his wattle.

He flies down to the parade for an inspection, preening himself, and pacing up and down in gentlemanly fashion to make sure you are presentable for visitors later in the day. While he walks he cranes his reciprocating neck, looking down your lines, checking for asymmetry, and picking up morsels of food; not one of you is out of step, not one of you is out of line, and he could find no fault with your uniforms, despite the years of marking time.

He approaches the shadow of the cross and bends over to touch the ground as a sign of respect, his tail sticking out like a sword beneath a greatcoat. NOTE 28 He ruffles his feathers; one falls gently to the stone surrounding the cross. He steps back looking straight ahead, his thoughts very much to himself.

On Commemoration Day in your hometowns, at the eleventh hour, on the eleventh day, on the eleventh month, your loved ones lay poppy-covered crosses below engraved monuments. They look at your ramrod straight backs, and read the ages on your uniforms; some of you barely babes out of arms. They will never know and understand the horror. How could they? Messages left enveloped in flimsy plastic coats become smudged and faded from sun and rain, and although indistinct and difficult to read, tell how they will forever miss and love you. Flowers laid at your feet indicating life and beauty soon shrivel, their legs cut from below them in their prime. Between your ranks stand begonias girded in their dark coats, unicoloured wreaths around their necks; they act as pallbearers. They have attended the ceremony for some time, replaced in their task every year. When wind blows, and rain lashes down dripping off their waterproof coats, they stalwartly march on until the end of their natural life; a life that has not been shortened prematurely, despite losing part of their wreath in a storm.

Germany commemorates the anniversary of the end of WWII with ceremonies and speeches in parliament emphasising German responsibility for a war that turned Europe into a mass graveyard. [5]

> In opposition across the parade ground of commemoration, stands a fellow unknown member of the human race – 'Ein Deutscher soldat', 'Known Only Unto God' – who was on the side that started this cataclysm but lost in the gigantic game of lobbing lumps of metal filled with explosives at each other. He stares dolefully at you through unblinking eyes, marching to try to stand at your shoulder but only attaining this in spirit. He lost, and you lost, because minutes before your extermination you had to kill him or die yourself. It never got easier, but you became more detached from what you were doing in your fight for existence; your comrades had to do the same. You fought battles for survival against annihilation, gunned by men at the top of the chain of command. Did his loved ones love him any less than yours because he was on the side of the aggressor? They, and a few of the members of the German armed forces, one an ace fighter pilot, thought that there was an invasion of their country, and Hitler was their saviour. They could not understand the lunacy, had they had any say they certainly would not have let it happen.

> You are safe from vandalism, apart from the elements, in this hallowed earth where the timeless march goes on. No hooligans shall defile this sacred ground or daub your pristine uniforms with their words of wisdom – none of their peers would set foot

on this revered land to see the result of their work. Then, you begged for escape from excitement, from the din and the thought of death, now they have to make excitement because they have nothing better to occupy their minds than nihilistic notions of nothingness. Their courage in attack arises from superiority in numbers, strength, weapons, or the element of surprise, their goal wanton destruction, death, or financial gain.

Your death has achieved peace; you have given all, one cog in the ponderous monster that lumbered across countries creating a path of devastation. You did not live to see that beyond this dark abyss in history through which the human race travelled, lay a sunlit plateau of tranquillity, peace, and ultimate beauty for some of humankind whose path led away from three of the Horsemen of the Apocalypse: War, Famine and Death. A gentle breeze stirs leaves and branches making them dance like marionettes; shadows flicker across some of your faces, a portent for future strife.

Autumn marches into winter; the solar elevation lowers, shortening the days. NOTE 29

> Autumn leaves come tumbling down,
> And old winter shows his face,
> His beard of white a pattern,
> Of delicate frosted lace.
> The winds of change blow through the trees,
> And time drifts gently on the breeze,
> Time that for you will never end,
> But time that will forever send,
> God's will held in his hand,
> Ripples through this hallowed land.

A EULOGY TO ABSENT FRIENDS

There are few visits to the cemetery, which becomes a silent, solitary place. The metabolism of organisms shuts down when the temperature falls, until the spring sun's radiation warms the air, when new life appears after apparent death. The sun barely drags itself out of bed and crawls lazily across the horizon, labouring less against its inclination as it apparently moves across the sky, its obliquity a manifestation of its lack of interest in earthly matters at this latitude; the lengthening shadows from your outlines trace their well-trodden arcs across the grass. It bids you farewell for the day; those of you at the front sheltering those at the back from the blinding rays, and slips below the horizon; darkness descends while you prepare for the forced marches through the night. The moon shines on the phalanx reflecting its luminosity, and from the surrounding hills your memorials look like spectral lines. A gentle dusting of snow creates a 'white out', your uniforms merging with small drifts that form at your feet; footprints are rarely seen at this time of the year when the parade is frozen in time.

Grey clouds scud across troubled skies, wind shakes hedgerows naked, tossing and twisting their leaves, which crumble to the dust of life to be born somewhere, sometime into new life forms from the molecules of existence. Snow falls on snow, snow on virgin snow, flake on fractal, feathery flake, layer on lingering layer, tilting up and down, rotating, settling gently on the ground, covering your feet, creeping up your legs, and dampening the sound of your marching. It comes down in an endless dream out of a sullen, leaden sky, and settles on your shoulders, softening your features, but adding nothing to your burden. It blunts the sharpness of your barbed, naked, stunted guardians, the purity covering your epaulettes – no black powder flash shall blemish your upstanding characters again. It is driven against the windward side of trees and dislodged from shivering branches. When it is powdered it funnels in and sprays out through a breach in a wall forming an expanding ridge, falling away in a graceful curve of nature. Flurries impelled against your chests fill the chiselled furrows on them, but the warmth of the message from your loved ones always burns through these non – duplicable crystals of the water of life.

A hedgehog, woken early from hibernation by lumps of snow falling off branches, pokes its nose out of the entrance to its den. Sniffing the air, which has no appetising smells, it realises its mistake and retreats rapidly with a grunt to warmer depths. When clouds clear and the sun pours its energy onto icicles, the melting water drills holes in the snow. It filters through the trees, casting long shadows over your graves and reflects off the snow giving your memorials a warm, pink hue. Birds sing a few dejected notes over the parade wondering how long it will be until spring returns. Another day ends, and stars appear in the stillness of the night.

Solidified streams of tears forming icicles sparkling in the sun run down your faces, across your chests, and reach down to encrust the message; the cold fingers soothe your anguish by anointing the words that you carry into eternity. When the heat of the sun warms your chests it melts the decorations that adorn the uniforms you wear with so much pride, and water runs down freely when you cease to be frozen by inhibition.

Ice crackles on the crust of frosted snow, wind scattering it at your feet, and clouds chase across the sky causing alternating brightness and darkness. A few blades of grass, which are sheltered and not yet dead, shake like frenetic batons conducting a sluggish orchestra, the music provided by branches and evergreen foliage that bend in supplication to you, making dancing shadows on your gravestones. Wisps of smoke rise from a coal fire, the smell evocative of a steam train and the immense power that humankind harnesses for beneficial purposes. NOTE 30

> A robin, red upon its chest,
> First year fledgling from the nest,
> A solitary snowflake upon its head,
> Sings about the beauty and silence,
> And makes myriad deformed crosses,
> Searching for food in the snow.
>
> She flies to a gravestone,
> And views the engraved messages,
> Which wear a beard of white.
> She knocks the snow from your epaulettes,
> And hops across them chirping a tune
> In time with your silent marching.
>
> At Christmas she sees a woman come
> And stare lovingly at the parade.
> Perched on your shoulder,
> Head cocked, with a quizzical look,
> She sees water running down her cheeks
> Not frozen by the cold.
> She does not understand what it means,
> But knows those who feed her
> Will not scare her away.

Standing on a headstone viewing the parade,
She wonders why so many humans are kind to her,
But kill each other for no good reason.
The killing she did was for survival,
Hard though it was in deep mid-winter.

She flits to a fir tree,
A standard bearer in the throng,
With its livery of evergreen;
No guardian angel on top,
No lights to guide your souls home,
No presents to lie at its feet,
No families of your loved ones
Gathered round with smiles and joy,
While they exchange presents in reunion.

Beneath a snowy blanket lies an unborn hope,
That flowers will bloom again at your frozen feet.
The robin sings of spring and the birth of new life;
She will take the snow with her and let you thaw in peace.

Chapter 6

Here lies a man of the cloth, whose clothes were left in tatters when he was killed by a stray shell that hit an advance field hospital, while ministering to the dying and dead. His dog collar was not lost, but his life was as surely as if he had been in battle. His words of comfort were succour to you when he reminded you of the nicer side of human nature, of the traits that most men have that balance the wickedness of the few. He impressed on you that as a saviour of your country your sacrifice would not be in vain, and you would be forgiven for your sins. But he asked himself why the immorality had continued to happen throughout history.

Men had been waging war for thousands of years but never learned the lesson of their folly. Could a nation turn the other cheek and be ruled by another nation? The other cheek had not been turned in countries where people worshipped other gods, when imperialistic rule had been imposed on them, and pecuniary profit had taken priority over human life, one episode in man's inhumanity to man. Hundreds of thousands of black people were taken from their homelands, transported by boat in conditions no better than a sewer, fed on a rat's diet and sold as slaves to empower whites in their bid for wealth with other nations.

By night the dark satanic forces circled probing his defences, trying to entice him into evil and give way to temptation. He awoke with a start, girding himself for the mental battle with the antichrist that uttered unmentionable profanities, and spat out rhetorical questions. How many deaths of heretics had there been in the name of interpretation of Christianity, and how many had been ostracised and burned for sorcery? How many mortals of opposing religious denominations were sent to their deaths for blasphemy? Had not nobility glorified war as a justification of their power, practising the promulgation of it rather than preaching the piety of peace? How many crusades had there been to the Holy Lands by those who believed their faith was everlasting?

In the dark ages, how many wars had there been for possession of land space and plunder, the landlords receiving redemption by giving to the Church? How many gentry, who had applied force of arms, acquired a plenary indulgence that freed them from the terrors of purgatory and hell, and provided salvation for their souls? How much adulation had there been for fighting for freedom of speech, and the liberty to follow the doctrine of your choice without denunciation? How often had the Inquisition, consciences never racked with guilt, tortured non-believers on the rack? How many wars had there been between countries to impose their religious beliefs on countries that had different religious followings, wars that lasted for years. NOTE 31

During his prayers he fought the unholy directives of the devil incarnate that had started this war. He morally armed his spirit to fight its telepathic powers, and pondered on the vexed question of the soul on the Day of Judgement. The beast is within us all – suppressed, held in check, and tempered by self-control. Nevertheless, free will can release it, and let it emerge in primeval form in an ascent through avarice to power.

In his devotions he tried to distil the essence of humanity. The actors on the stage of life's short show must learn their lines for the acts of diplomacy to prevent man's end point – extinction – to forget them means taking a downward path into oblivion. They must look for new horizons, surfing the continuum of life in their search for the deeper truths – communication, conciliation, and mediation – in a climb to a higher plane of understanding and spiritual peace. They should plumb the depths of the well of human benevolence that is unfathomable, most of us dabbling at the surface. They have to reach down to find the rich tapestry of emotions waiting and needing to be explored in this selfish world of take with little give, where there are so many of us less well-off materially and emotionally bereft. They require the help of those with compassion who can afford to give it, but unfortunately there are not enough who think about it and give from the bottom of their hearts that very feminine of emotions – love.

When in philosophical mood during a short service, his words of wisdom rang true. 'Some of us make our own way through life, we search our souls, pick over the rubble, and tinker with it to try to build ourselves a dream that we hope will come to fruition; some of us never discover ourselves, never find the truth through self – exploration, and are lead through life; some of us take away the enlightenment and happiness that others have found, leaving their lives in ruin, depending on friendship and kindness from others to rebuild them. You owe your life to the earth below your feet; your debt can never be repaid until you return there; you cannot take any credit with you. But on your journey you can help to repay your debts and offset material sins by acts of kindness to others who have raised from the same earth and who you will join as neighbours. Your soul will be with those to whom you showed kindness – human life is sacred'.

At the final roll call The Redeemer looks inside our souls and chooses those bound for hell. They descend the downward path to perdition following a rake's progress after a lifetime of cruelty and inconsideration. Those not singled out ascend the slope to the eternal afterlife after receiving absolution for a lifetime of mercy and consideration.

At the end he comforted you on behalf of your loved ones, sadly not at home or due to natural causes. He prayed, 'let there be peace on Earth between all mankind'. In the hospital, which was a converted church, the words 'Gloria in excelcis deo' (Glory to God on high) had been written on the roof. This small building existed for the glorification of god as much as a massive cathedral.

In his prayers he pleaded with the omniscient, omnipotent power to stop the insanity; they were answered, but not before he too succumbed to the machinations of the devil. The cloth enshrouded him forever at the end of his days of showing pity to those tortured souls who lay before him.

> Our genes and evolution,
> Have made us what we are,
> And our ultimate purpose,
> Means it is hard to avoid war.

For our ultimate purpose is
Survival and procreation,
But violence is in our nature,
Not just our imagination.

In our search for land space,
And wealth and material gain,
We violate the human race,
And all Earth creatures' names.

It was Christmas Eve, and with a heavy heart the village priest trudged through deepening snow past the headstones with their white overcoats, hunched against a blinding blizzard, his default countenance – absence. His boots made firm impressions in the snow, which collected above his collar and scarf, freezing his neck. It weighed down evergreen branches, bending them until the snow fell off, and they sprung back again. He had been offering Midnight Mass after visiting some of his congregation who could not get to church. The Christmas tree lights in houses guided his way through the snowstorm. Presents were laid out on the eve of the birth of Christ; excited children hoping they would see Santa Claus – the personification of Christmas.

Earlier, having served Vespers (the evening prayers) he listened to the confessions of two men. One, contrite for his venial sins, admitted he had lost his belief; 'Forgive me Father, for I have sinned'. He gave him absolution, cleansing his soul for misdeeds, apparent truths, and untruths. The other, a reprobate, had searched his soul and found it wanting; he had discovered his spirit to be a vast, vacant void in limbo between temporal wealth and immaterial poverty. While listening, his thoughts aligned the tumblers of his mind, releasing the secrets of his soul. He deliberated on the depravity of the souls and the mortal sins committed by a few of his colleagues, and the financial irregularities of one, a priest called Monsignor Cinquecento because he carried five hundred euro notes with him. We all have demons and want to confront them, to live a better way. We don't know if we will be forgiven, but we hope we will, and be able to RIP. Some of us come to terms with our demons, some of us live in a constant battle with good living side by side with them, never overcoming them but being forgiven at the end, and some of us live with them never knowing forgiveness. NOTE 32

The priest replied that the bleakness of the soul could be enriched by acts of altruism, and it was possible to be given an indulgence and admitted to purgatory if reparation was made for ones sins. He berated himself for forgetting to order more votive candles; he had been busy. A woman attended daily to light one and pray for the safety of her relatives in a war zone a continent away. She said there was no need to apologise for we are all forgiven on the day of reckoning. He deliberated on the question of women joining the clergy, and the historical reasoning that was being considered; he felt that they should because their biological makeup was different from males. Female attributes embrace love, caring, nurture, friendship and connection, which are at the core of the Christian doctrine.

He understood the darkness of the souls of the spiritually bereft. His brother had been a steadfast atheist who had had his own belief system; he had not believed in confession and absolution for sins that might be repeated again; he had not accepted that prayer would alter his future. He had never been in contact with God and had not had faith in him. His polemic against Christianity centred on the doctrine of Holy Trinity.

The priest mulled over the Faith Communities on Earth, and how they had fought against each other when their belief in a god, friendship and peace, and equality between humankind was the same. He prayed that wisdom would be found – but where? We are sentient – well, most of us are. Those of us who are not are incapable of sharing friendship and showing compassion; they are insensitive and have no feelings. They are born into countries where rule is by patriarchal political systems, which create so much misery and death. We are born, we live, and we die – there is no hurry to get to the end – we take nothing with us: we leave only memories.

> It drew near on a midnight bright,
> When your souls were at low ebb,
> A star of great luminosity,
> Shone brightly overhead.
>
> In that great enlightenment,
> Your spirits were set free,
> To search for your loved ones,
> As free as free could be.
>
> To look for peace on Earth,
> Concord between humankind,
> The salvation of humanity,
> This redemption you must find.

A farmer, his forehead a furrowed frown, makes his way across a snow-covered field dotted with craggy rock outcrops and evergreen broom, his collie following him faithfully. He pauses to view the parade, which is a palette of white on a landscape of white. Consternation creases his face and condensation carries on his breath, his thoughts of the infinite, uninhabited, vacuum that war creates, and the beauty of nature.

He crosses a farm track covered by ice formed by freezing temperatures overnight. Along the verge a forest of frozen ferns have donned their copper coloured coats for winter. Some are bent over and crippled, some erect and strong, waiting for the cold to disintegrate their structures. An insipid sun shines on the snowy scene; berries on trees covered in a furry, icy layer wait to fall to the ground or be eaten by birds; one of them might take root, and progress through its long journey of growth.

The dog looks up at his master's perplexed countenance, and seeing his anguish pushes his nose into his master's hand and licks it. For several minutes the farmer stands lost in thought, tears in his eyes; grateful for his companionship he rubs the dog's head.

He crosses a field veiled with a light covering of snow; stubble sticks up through it waiting to be recycled into the ground to keep humanity alive. Sheep waiting for food look at him and the dog with blank, expressionless faces, unaware of the impending slaughter of their children.

Across the valley a line of skeletal, gangling, grey, metal structures march across the countryside, straddling roads and rivers in one leap, and climbing hills in staggered arrays. Their three pairs of arms are bent at right angles at the elbows, their forearms vertical strings of insulating ceramic discs, their hands clasping conductors that carry the force, and two bracelets around their wrists. NOTE 33 On a hill up the valley stands a sentry, an obelisk, a four-sided monument ending in a pyramidal top, which in two of the Egyptian dynasties was a cult symbol of Ra, the sun god and creator of all. For a short time in the year, when the sun rises over the summit of the hill, the top of the church spire is struck by the shadow of the tip of the obelisk, which follows a straight road lined by triumphal poplar trees as the sun ascends. Nearby, a folly has been erected; it was built to pretend to be the remains of a building – a monument to man's folly. NOTES 34/35

In the distance on the battleground, the fields are ploughed and the seed scattered, the crops grow to their full stature, ripening to a golden brown, and are gathered from the very soil on which you died. The parade keeps watch, waiting for the return of your souls from their eternal search for peace in humanity.

Here time stands still for you, your gaze fixed across the placid waters of the lake, the breeze rustling through the trees: what secrets lie within its depths when man was ill at ease? The tide of our aspirations will forever ebb and flow, the measure be ever so slow, the seeds of doubt implanted in our minds, the shoots of faith so difficult to find. Cesspits of evil are drained by good will, vast tracts of desolation flood with friendship. Fallow, once fertile fields of forgotten feelings – the sterile soil once more impregnated with promise – are swamped by swathes of grass and grain, flourishing in the sunlight into a surfeit of concord and happiness.

The seasons of our hope will ever change, the colours of our future be rearranged. Some of us entered an autumn of shortening days when night closed in on any enlightenment; violence, destruction and death, accompanied by change of colour and wrinkling of fallen foliage, were followed by a winter of cold, darkness, discontent and obliteration. Some of us entered a spring of lengthening days, when new life blossomed in all its ways, and kindness, love and peace burgeoned into a summer of brightness, warmth, content and infinite beauty.

We come to visit this island awash in a sea of sadness, within a paradise, ever hopeful that the divine wisdom in life will be attained. We take away the memory of you in all your grandeur with ramrod straight backs, suitably humbled by the experience, in awe that so many could give their lives without question.

> You gave so much and expected so little,
> Now we expect so much and give so little.

Another day comes to an end; the sun appears to kiss the Earth goodnight, light leaves the day behind, the moon shines on the phalanx reflecting its luminosity, and from the surrounding hills your memories look like spectral lines.

Chapter 7

Here lies an aviator, who fought with comrades in the Battle of Britain. He was woken at six o'clock by his batman, who maintained his uniform and acted as a valet, and joined his friends to eat breakfast in the mess. They snoozed in the summer sun for a minute or two, waiting until the middle of the day for the German planes to appear, but mostly living on their nerves, joking with friends, putting a face on things, and waiting for the call to 'scramble'.

When the call came through on the tannoy, he ran to his Spitfire, climbed into the cockpit, and was strapped in with the help of one of his ground crew. He set the elevator trim and rudder bias, checked the brakes were on, turned the fuel cock on, set the throttle mixture, switched on the ignition switches, and pressed the starter and coil boost buttons – contact; he fired up the V12 Rolls Royce Merlin engine. It coughed, cleared its throat, flames and smoke blew out of its six exhausts as oil was cleared from the cylinders, and roared into life, settling to a growling idle. He checked his instruments and control surfaces and took off in a flight of three, climbing to 11,000 feet in the cornflower blue sky filled with cumulus. They were alerted by 'ops' that there were 'bandits, angels twelve', and climbed to get above them, seeing the carpet of bombers and escorting fighters through broken cloud.

They dived out of the sun and the flight split up; two dived on two Me109s that had been given a shouted warning over their intercoms, one breaking into a right turn. One of the Spitfires followed but was too close to get inside the enemy's turn; the Me109 continued its turn and then banked to the left. The Spitfire continued flying in a semi-circle and they approached each other at the speed of sound; they passed, both breaking to the left. They made several circles but the Spitfire's superior speed and tighter turn rate enabled it to catch up with the German. Suddenly the German climbed and performed a defensive barrel roll to slow his speed, pulling to the left, then to the right, slowing even more. The Spitfire was not far enough behind and overshot. The German was now behind the Spitfire; he pushed his engine to maximum revolutions, and when he got in range started firing. The Spitfire shuddered as a few cannon shells hit the airframe. Its pilot rolled, pulled into a turn, levelled, pulled back hard on the stick, and went into a steep climb. The Me109 followed, but its climb rate was less than the Spitfire's because of a slight loss of power when it arrived over England, and the German couldn't get it in his sights. The Me109 reached its peak altitude in that attitude for the power output from its engine, its power to weight ratio being less than the Spitfire's, shuddered and went into an uncontrolled stall. The Spitfire attained a higher altitude and the pilot was able to turn into a controlled dive before the plane stalled, and was now on the Me109's tail; he fired a burst, seeing tracer hit the plane. The German tried to pull out of his dive having regained control of the plane, but with the damage and his heavier controls he was unable to do so. The Spitfire pilot was grateful

A EULOGY TO ABSENT FRIENDS

that he had a sudden death, which he would have hoped for had he been hit.

The second Spitfire picked one of the other Me109s, closed, started firing at an angle of five o'clock, but missed. The German rolled and pulled back hard, but because his cockpit was smaller, his control column travel shorter, – almost reaching his chest – and his control surfaces heavier, needing more effort by his upper body muscles, he could not move the column as quickly as the Spitfire pilot. As a result, his roll and turn rate was slower, and as the Spitfire was not too close it came inside the German's turn and waited for him to come across his line of fire. However, his angle of deflection was incorrect and he missed.

> The German inverted, pulled back hard on the stick diving toward the ground, and performed a loop; coming out at the top he continued climbing. The Me109 was now above and behind another Spitfire, which applied left and right rudder, changing position, looking for enemy aircraft. The German dived at its six o'clock, a few bullets finding their target, leaving holes with fabric flapping over them. The Spitfire pilot throttled up, pulled right into a climbing turn then reversed, flipping to the left, and found the Me109 below and in front of him. He closed until he was in range and fired a 'blunderbuss' shot from his machine guns, peppering the Me109. The German pilot took evasive action; the Spitfire overshot and was in the Me109's sights. The Spitfire pilot pulled back the stick to just above a stall, stood on the pedal, the rudder went

hard over, the plane slewed round, and as the Me109 passed him he fired a blind burst. The German went into a dive trailing smoke from burning oil; it turned over and he saw a parachute blossom out when the pilot bailed out over the sea.

The third Spitfire picked one of the fighters and gave a long burst hitting its wing; it turned over and fell towards the ground – cannon shells hit the Spitfire's fuselage. The pilot pulled back the stick and climbed 2,000 feet, entering cloud for a short time, but when he came out the German had guessed where he might exit and was still above and behind him. He flew in a steep turn to the right, and as the airframe shimmied at the point of stall he hoped that the enemy would fall out of his own turn. Unfortunately, due to damage to an aileron, he crossed the German's sights briefly and was hit by a few shells. He pulled the stick hard back stalling the Spitfire, gave full bottom rudder to drop the nose, the torque of the propeller turned the plane anticlockwise, and pushed the stick forward neutralising the effect; the air speed dropped virtually to zero, the plane dropped vertically for 2,000 feet until it picked up air speed and recovered from its stall, evading the German.

A Spitfire crossed the sights of a Me109 diving out of the sun, but the German missed because the deflection angle was incorrect. The Spitfire pilot took skidding evasive action, twisting and turning, applying right and left rudder but the Me109 closed. He made a steep dive to see if he could out run him, but since he was unable to nose down immediately, because there was fuel starvation to the carburettors when negative 'g' forces were pulled, he had to make a roll falling into a dive to overcome it. The Me109 had fuel injection and the pilot pushed up the power, closed rapidly, and fired a burst: only a few shells hit the fuselage. The Spitfire pulled out of its dive before the plane started vibrating, pulled hard right into a 90-degree turn, which was like locking the brakes on a car, and levelled.

The German, whose plane was heavier and could not pull out of a dive so quickly, overshot, levelled and was below and in front of him. He managed to fire off a few shots but missed. The German performed a scissors manoeuvre, rolling and pulling to the right, reversing and pulling to the left, and climbing, bringing him to the six o'clock position behind the Spitfire; he overshot because he was approaching too quickly. The German pulled hard to the left and then to the right, climbing, getting behind him again, and fired a short burst. The Spitfire pilot pushed the throttle through the gate, the supercharger engaged, the plane shuddered, the engine howled as air was rammed into the carburettors giving a leap in power and speed; he tried to outrun the German in a dive.

Approaching the ground he pulled back the stick, which was heavy and sluggish, but there was only a small reduction in the angle of descent since there was damage to an aileron. He pulled back harder and harder, but his plane continued its descent. The area was hilly and he aimed for a valley to give him more time to come out of his dive, pulling round in a long turn to try to lose some speed; there was minimal response and when he entered the valley he was just about flying level. He approached a turn in the river, and unable to negotiate it he ploughed into a hillside. NOTE 36

Women worked in the armed forces in non-combative roles, delivering fighters from factories to airfields; some test flew new planes. The Women's Auxiliary Air Force manned radar stations tracking incoming bombers, a dangerous job since they were often bombed. The Woman's Territorial Service acted as drivers, cleaned, and worked in mess halls where they had to peel potatoes. They manned anti-aircraft guns but Churchill forbade them to fire because he felt they would not be able to cope with the knowledge they had killed young German men; they were, however, allowed to track a plane, fuse the shells and be present when the gun was fired. During the 'Battle of Britain' posters were put up echoing Churchill's never to be forgotten words:

'NEVER HAS SO MUCH BEEN OWED BY SO MANY TO SO FEW'

The Air Raid Protection Force (ARP) enforced the 'Blackout', making sure no light shone from house windows. Persistent offenders, who allowed it to escape, were taken in front of Magistrates. Some of the women in the force volunteered to drive ambulances, taking people with minor injuries to first aid posts, and more seriously injured ones to hospital: the dead were taken to mortuaries. Shrapnel, rather than bomb blast, caused many injuries.

Women in the Women's Voluntary Service were 'Jacks of all trades'. They supplied tea and refreshments to firemen and people sheltering in the Underground stations, and collected light scrap metal. They looked after people who had lost their loved ones, and items of clothing were knitted for servicemen. We must never forget the sacrifice made both by combatants and non-combatants in this war; never forget that we could be dictated to by a Fascist state and speaking German as our first language; never forget that the German people were freed from rule by a dictator. Would this state have been magnanimous towards us?

> Spring flowers push up their shoots,
> And send a message to their roots.
> The photon drive has returned,
> With water we will not be burned.
> H+ protons sucked into a wheel,
> Are bound to phosphate in a deal,
> ADP to ATP it sells,
> And energises our dormant cells.
> On a bent axle merry-go round,
> We'll rise up from the fertile ground.

NOTE 37

Spring walks away from winter, days lengthen, the sun's radiation warms the air, and new life rises once more from Mother Earth in its annual cycle of death and resurrection. Lambs frolic in the fields, their master full of good cheer. You stretch your muscles, and straighten and dust your uniforms in anticipation of the forthcoming inspections, and appreciation of your sacrifice.

The sun rises out of the shadows of dawn at the behest of the pallid moon, it takes precedence, and flowers start to bloom. Daffodil buds push up towards their source of energy supported by strong stalks; they grow through spring, their buds opening to reveal petals that form a hat. Clusters of them toss their heads and laugh in an optimistic dance. A storm of snowdrops shivers and bends in the breeze that blows the sighing of souls through the parade. Their cowls of virginal white droop with the accumulated grief, but their sturdy legs do not bow under the force, and as the melting snow drips at their feet it lightens their load. An assumption of crocuses that the sun would always shine on them proved correct, a tapestry of purple, yellow and white banked towards it in a riot of tricolour. When they are exposed to the elemental energy of creation they take water and nutrients from soil to produce new bulbs, and their petals dehisce cyclically. By night, when there is no radiation of power from the sun, their petals close as if praying for your souls. You watch as hyacinths, having lain dormant over winter, are rejuvenated, and wish that you could be; their heavy scent drifts, guiding your relatives on their pilgrimages. NOTE 38

Spring merges into summer, cherry blossom leading the welcome; the parade marches into extinction. The sun climbs higher above the horizon daily, the Earth circling it on its yearly journey, and gently kisses your foreheads, cheeks and lips, bringing warmth and colour to them, enlightening with illumination your epitaphs. It wakes another day full of promise for peace: hope springs perpetual, doubt ever vanquished.

In high summer, when the sun shows a deep desire for closeness to the cemetery, and radiates all its affection at full power, the grass around where you lie, and where some of you fell, dries out. Fountains of tears spring from the ground when your souls cry for peace, splashing your white, Earthbound relics, wetting your faces, showing that even in death your emotions show from features of stone, and watering your companions, the flora, in the flower of their youth. NOTE 39

> Come the dawn when the mists have gone,
> And the birds sing their daily prayers.
> You stand side by side,
> With the sun in your eyes,
> As the day marches along by your sides.

Birds chirp and chatter in the trees, on the slopes of flowing fields, flowers stream and hiss. A firm breeze filters through the cemetery fondling tree blossom, making it shake, dance and drop. Its purpose served, it blows across the parade ground – a snowstorm in summer – making a speckled carpet of confetti at the marriage of the messenger blossom of life and Earth. It tracks across the smooth step around the cross forming piles on the sheltered side. Your souls clutch at it, carrying it down to the ground to be reunited with your bodies; it lies at rest, shrivelling, once more returning to earth from whence it came. On breathless days you stand erect despite the sweltering heat. There is tranquillity, but elsewhere in the world conflict continues. In the distance a shimmering mirage forms an impressionistic haze of pastel colours.

> On bright and cloudless days,
> When the sun cannot hide,
> Slender stalked carnations,
> Parade their stylish hats,

To those who venture by.
There is no loss of continuity,
As time goes marching on,
Another days comes to an end,
But have we all moved on?

Within sight of your consecrated ground, legion upon legion of poppies march, bending their heads in the breeze in deference. They have seen many of you fall on the same ground in centuries gone by, never to rise again; your blood spattered them darker red, and many fell with you. They will be with you for diuturnity, respecting your sacrifice for your fellow men, and protecting you.

Where you fell and came to rest,
Poppies grew on your chests.
Although you were dug in deep,
They did not bring you peaceful sleep.

On and on for endless days,
They swayed in the breeze.
In heat, and drought, they marched
To cold, and chill, and freeze.

They had seen raw grief and sadness,
And how the world went wrong.
Will they still be alive?
When centuries are passed down?

Will they watch over the parade?
Or will they become extinct,
Because of selfish man?

When their annuities end their vibrant coloured petals fade in the sun, wither, and perish, scattering their opium-laden seeds to rejuvenate Mother Earth. In summer, many will take root and grow into an adult, and on into old age, a position denied to you. In times gone by they enriched creativity, in the present they cause a perverse addiction that can lead to a lifetime of crime.

When they fall they pass into the afterlife, arising from your graves to flower again. They stand guard over you and the messages from your loved ones, and bring you eternal rest. As time goes by, individually you may be forgotten: as one you will not – will humanity learn its lesson?

A bird flies over one of the many regular shaped areas of grass with parallel dotted white lines on them that look like green pages from a book. It checks its bearings and adjusts its course, grateful for the navigational aids that are plentiful in this part of the country. Despite the noise of battle birds could be heard singing when the shelling stopped.

Dazzling sunspots dance on your sleeves through fluttering leaves, and feather tailed cirrus creeps across the sky cooling your foreheads. Shafts of diverging sunlight shine through breaks in the cloud, bathing the surrounding countryside with swathes of brilliance. Dandelion seeds float on the breeze over wheat fields, and settle on the earth to multiply.

A gardener tends the soil around your graves, removing weeds that grow aggressively, which stifle beautiful, delicate plants. He snips the dead heads of roses, which will grow again next year from the elements of the earth and air, and cuts the grass, making two shades of green running parallel to your ranks. When your headstones move a few degrees from the vertical they are repositioned, and you are once again in line with your colleagues and march in unison.

He is an elderly man who enjoys his work, and keeps a steady pace despite suffering pain from war injuries. He takes a rest from digging and stands in the shelter of a tree; his thoughts rise from the ground to an elevated state and he ponders on the meaning of life. Some of us lead a sedentary existence expecting everything to fall into our laps without offering anything in return – the culture of instant gratification. Some of us plod on a treadmill, never going or getting anywhere, stuck in a self-perpetuating cycle. Some of us steer our own way through life taking a direct route, vaulting the hurdles and avoiding the pitfalls. Some of us evade the hurdles, taking a zigzag course, trying to miss the pot holes and barriers, sometimes falling in but managing to pull ourselves out, and sometimes needing help from others. Some of us trip over the first hurdle or disappear down the first hole on the path, and are unable to get out even with help from others, stagnating for the rest of our lives.

> The sun is split by the horizon,
> And a flight of geese on the wing.
> Light and dark cut by reality,
> And the sinking of the golden ring.

On hot evenings the soporific scent of jasmine hangs heavily, anaesthetising your tortured souls, and sending them into a slumber. The smell of new cut hay lingers in the air, and the plodding of a herd of cows can be heard as they instinctively wander home to be milked. Your souls drift across the parade ground trying to console one another – some of you have no living relative to visit you.

The sun moves down painting the sky a hint of rose, and when it hovers above the horizon the grain glows golden; it strolls through trees and sinks, lengthening their shadows: twilight gathers. The Earth embraces it, goodnight: the moon appears a ghostly circle on ethereal blue.

> Below a moonlit sky,
> Lay a silver lake,
> Where ducks taking off,
> Left their rippled wake.

Crafty old Reynard returned home some considerable time after the battle, his beard greying with the sagacity born of need, his wiliness born of necessity in the life he had to lead. He found a battery of foxholes that were palaces where he could earth his new vixen and cubs.

Despite his wiles he had not managed to lead his family to safety before the bombardment started, returning from a foray for food to find a vast crater in the earth where his den had been. After the war had ended he came back to a desert that man had made, his campaign to re-inhabit it about to start. In an uninhabitable desert across a sea an army's battle had come to an end; the Desert Rats had done their cornering rather than vice versa, and the Desert Fox had been defeated. NOTES 40/41

The slyness of his species was sometimes not enough to escape the baying executors of man; they had to face the packed enemy alone after the howling mob was laid with no protection from an army. Badgers hiding in their sets until nightfall were sometimes set upon by mistake. Despite being a predator that had to be kept under control, their furs were paraded in society by the very society that killed them.

His ancestor sticks his black snout out through the camouflage of a bush: laid in the direction of approaching prey, condensed breath issues from it in the still air. It traverses left and right waiting to ambush them, his stealth a requirement for his survival, his nonchalant air belying his cunning. This did not extend to crossing roads at night when he might be killed because he was unaware of the speed of oncoming traffic, despite the noise of cars and the glare of their headlights.

There were no urban foxes during the war; food was in short supply. Everything was eaten or recycled, vegetable peelings made into soup, and other food waste fed to farm animals – nothing was thrown away. Sandwiches filled with 'dripping' were eaten – nearly all of the population were the ideal weight, although they were hungry. NOTES 42/43

The government introduced rationing to ensure everyone had a fair share of what was available and every man, woman and child was given a ration book. The local community had to register with their grocer; he was supplied with enough food to feed them. When food was bought the shopkeeper stamped the ration book. Children bought sweets using a blue ration book. When they were purchased the storekeeper tore a coupon out – their weekly ration. Potatoes were not rationed; the local chip shop was open at weekends, which was a great treat. Clothes were rationed due to a shortage of raw material and the population required coupons to buy them. The nation was encouraged to 'make do and mend', to repair or patch torn or worn clothes. The wheels had to be taken off cars to disable them: petrol was rationed and not for private use.

A walker ambles along a country path towards the cemetery where a friend of her son is buried, passing below the expansive canopy of a beech tree. The ground below is covered with dead leaves, which have not disintegrated since the previous winter: the sweet smell of honeysuckle wafts on the breeze. She comes upon a pool that reflects the sun, making her screw up her eyes to shade them, and sits down. A water boatman skis across the pool, the surface tension of the water supporting it. A coot carries insects to its open mouthed young, who jostle for position to be fed, in a nest in the reeds. Her mate dives to the bottom of the pool to collect weeds and comes up metres away, shaking water off its feathers. A frog sits on a boulder, croaking anxiously; waiting expectantly for an insect to come in reach of its tongue, unaware of predators nearby. A dragonfly hovers, waiting to catch insects, its short life soon to be terminated by a fish lurking below the surface.

The breeze whispers to the grass to release its pollen, and carries the pungent smell of oil seed rape. The walker hears the noise of a cuckoo in the nearby wood, waiting for the opportunity for a female of a bird of another species to vacate its nest. When this happens she will fly to the nest and lay an egg, or if there is already one there, push it out before laying her own in the host nest.

She climbs over a style and skirts a meadow of wild flowers where there are clumps of rare snake's head fritillary with their widow's shawls of checked purple.

She lies down, the soporific effect of bees collecting nectar lulling her to sleep. She wakes with a start when a woodpecker starts hammering at a tree to get grubs under the bark. It has evolved adaptations to protect its brain, which is small and orientated to give maximum contact with its skull.

In late afternoon, she walks round an estate that has rhododendrons along its edge, finding foxgloves, and rose bay willow herb in disturbed ground: ahead lie ash trees, their leaves withering on the branch. When she nears the cemetery a gull passes overhead following the course of the river from the sea to the lake, and trailing behind the flight. The fish dropped from the nets of boats were less due to over fishing. Worms could be caught from fields that had been ploughed.

She makes her way home to cook a meal for her son who lost a leg in war. He is out with a fellow soldier, who had an arm amputated, giving support to a new amputee who was having difficulty coming to terms with his injury, had post-traumatic stress, had committed an act of violence and could see no way forward. She was grateful to have her son home.

She reminded him that some of us who had sunshine in our lives, who have been physically and emotionally abused, are left drifting in the dark, sailing against a head wind, and unable to make any decisions. Bereft of the sun we become crippled and limp, needing an emotional crutch from others to get through the storm. They deflect the wind, which veers through 180 degrees, and blows from behind clearing clouds, until the sun appears in our lives once more, and clarity in our minds.

Chapter 8

Swans dressed in puritanical plumage glide aloofly on the lake near the cemetery; their necks orange tipped question marks, hanging over man's assumed superiority in matters pertaining to nature, their supremacy shown by the serenity of their silence. They take off treading, and then running on water, gaining momentum until their speed is enough to attain lift against gravity. They ascend in a gentle slope forming a massive carpet, take a bearing using their compasses in their ears, and head for magnetic north.

On their northern flight path they see the beauty of the Aurora, the flashing luminosity reflecting the radiance of resonating atoms in their eyes. NOTE 44 In the past, their ancestors on their migration to and from warm lands – necessary for their survival – flew over a large area with many oblong buildings enclosed by wire. One, a crucible of conflagration with a tall chimney belching out smoke, lay along the axis of the enclosure; nearby there was a stationary iron monster that did the same.

A line of cattle wagons standing behind it spewed forth human beings in a state of utter exhaustion. They had been penned in and denied water on the long journey that lasted days; in winter they froze to death, in summer they dehydrated. They could not sit, but if they co-operated they could sit on each other's knees. The floors were awash with urine and excreta – dead bodies were piled up to make room for those left alive. A mother sat in the corner of a wagon hugging her screaming baby to her chest. She did not know where she was going, but hoped it would be better than the ghetto. They emerged into the daylight, falling, blinking, disorientated, questioning, confused, and terrified. Some were shot inside the trucks if they refused to get off, some when they got off: there was no respect for human life.

They formed a queue in front of an officer; the decision about their future was about to be made. Young men, and others fit enough to undertake hard labour, were sent to the right – the 'good' side. They had an ID number tattooed on their arms – their personal identity taken from them – a number in a killing machine. They walked through the gate at the entrance to the camp, which bore the motto 'Arbeit macht frei' (labour makes (you) free). Most children, woman, older men, and those who looked unfit and unhealthy were directed with a whip to the left – the 'evil' side – murdered immediately and piled ten deep: babies, young children, adults – all together. NOTE 45

Men, and women, in uniforms as black as a moonless night; with skewed aberrant crosses on them, who marched arrogantly like a close relative of the swans, hounded queues of men, women, and screaming children, battering them with their gun butts. NOTE 46 They endured despicable degradations while they shuffled in a downtrodden, obeisant state of abject fear towards a building where their executioners took everything from them: clothes, jewellery, spectacles, dolls and family photographs.

From this building they were taken down the 'Himmelstrasse' – 'the heavenly road' – and herded towards a gas chamber; a building with no windows that was camouflaged to keep the mass murder system secret from the victims. If they had known they were headed to their deaths they would have attacked the guards; they would have had nothing to lose. Instead, they meekly followed each other like lambs to the slaughter. They were packed so tightly inside, where they thought they were going to have a shower, that when they died there was no room to fall; their bodies had to be prised apart by their compatriots allocated the task of removal – it was killing on an industrial scale.

Their executioners then prised out their gold fillings and wrenched their gold rings off their fingers, placing them in piles that categorised their nature until assayed and secreted elsewhere; some were changed into currency and the money put into neutral country's banks. Items made of gold were smelted down and made into ingots.

Their jostling ghosts hovered at their death site, silent screams leaving the lips of their doleful, anguished faces. Their souls followed their hosts when their bodies were removed on trolleys, or pulled with giant tongs around their heads, to the building with the chimney – 'Dante's inferno'. Here they were piled up like sides of beef, and cremated in banks of ovens – the hourglass had run through – the next batch was driven in and exterminated.

In the crematorium the Grim Reaper, the personification of Death, divorced Life, and scythed their souls in an abrupt disengagement from their bodies, which turned to ash. Their souls, shocked by the sudden severance, and unable to stay with their hosts, drifted desolate at their loss of reunion with their bodies in resurrection; the Reaper ushered them into the afterlife. Their ashes were piled into a nearby river and marsh and used as fertilizer in nearby fields. Many were buried in mass graves: in death they further lost their identity. NOTE 47

The prisoners fit for hard labour worked sixteen hours a day, using their hands to claw at rocks if there were no implements. They slept four to a bunk with no room to lie on their backs; if one wanted to turn, everyone had to follow. There was one toilet for each block accommodating four hundred people. If they were lucky they were able to bathe once a week to wash away the smell of ordure. If there was dysentery, as there often was, their filth was scattered everywhere; they died from dehydration due to diarrhoea. Vermin lived side by side with the occupants, nestling beside the overflowing bucket of human waste that was used overnight. Around the perimeter of the compound there was a double electric fence; foxes smelling the rotting flesh electrocuted themselves when they tried to get through.

After months on a starvation diet, they began to deteriorate physically leading to a 'muselmann' state of extreme exhaustion, which ended in death. Some would walk through the huts giving their last scraps of bread to try to help the weak, often a pointless exercise because they were beyond help. Emaciation emasculated some of empathy for others in their bid for life; they were deflated bags of flesh and bone. Some threw themselves against electric fences, a quick, sure death. At roll call, 'Appell', the ones who died in the night were dragged out and counted along with the thousands of prisoners; if there were any mistakes in the count they were beaten by SS guards. They had to stand for hours; the weak shot or attacked by dogs if they dropped. If there was a penal call – a punishment for the misconduct of a prisoner – they stood all night in the freezing cold, and were thrashed and shot. Some prisoners who had been promoted and given special privileges by the SS, German convicts known as 'Kapos' carried out many duties involved in the genocide, but not the gassing. They beat their compatriots more ferociously than the Germans: they were murdered if they did not. Hundreds died by the week due to infection and malnutrition, piled like logs until reduced to ashes. The stench of death was continually present from dead bodies, and the burning of human flesh.

Chicken-legged skeletons stumbled along; some held up by another emaciated, shrivelled, pathetic shadow of a human being who looked like a rag-hung scarecrow. Some were bloated due to starvation, others mere shrunken skins, their ribs showing like furrows on a field, old fractures prominent like rocky outcrops. They were bereft of any emotion, which was flailed out of them by unimaginable cruelty, if the slightest flicker of it raised its head as a sign of temerity in that centre of hell. The last vestiges of humility hung in tatters with their clothes, their faith only covering their nakedness in the eyes of God, their bond fellows of the same religious following in the same situation. The men, and women, who perpetrated these barbaric crimes, enjoyed performing operations without anaesthesia on screaming men, women and children, and carried out experiments; lampshades were made from skin. They had parties outside, enjoying food and music while the holocaust went on.

They could not see the beauty of the world, only ugliness. Their lives had no meaning; there was no life in their lives: no birds, no flowers, and no grass, only rodents scuttling about. The time of their lives was coming to an end: the arrow of time became existence. The watch hand turned in indication, but the winder never revolved in optimism, the spring was never wound up in hope, and the teeth never engaged in anticipation of escape from the endless barbarity. They could not show any more pain; they could feel it mentally, but not show it externally. Their facial expressions were fixed masks of tragedy, their brains depleted emotionally by the constant abuse; they had endured suffering for so long that the well was dry: their tears had dried up. Their bodies, habituated to the constant denigration, could not trigger the physical response. The emotional pendulum had stopped swinging, fixed at the bottom of its arc, but the endless torrent of inhumanities and bestiality inflicted on the poor wretches, who were treated worse than animals, never stopped. A perpetual stream of brutality rained down, crushing all recognition of being out of them. They survived as automata; they took in what little food and water they could get. They had shut out the belief that human beings could treat them in any other way. There was no other way for them as they staggered towards oblivion. The souls of some ascended to that exalted place, the astral plane. They left their bodies and reached a serene state where they could exclude the horrors, remember enjoyable times with their loved ones, and look on their captors as animals to be treated with disdain.

There was an endless continuum of days without respite, when they were pulverised to a pitiful pulp and kicked out of the way like a despised dog. With no resilience left it was not possible to bounce back from despair – could they ever trust a fellow human being again? Some entertained no thoughts of forgiveness, despite their religious teachings; they had borne wretchedness beyond belief.

They did not believe that their star would rise again to shine down on them leading them to safety and their promised land. The sun had set long ago on this charnel house and conveyor belt of combustion in the eyes of the inhabitants. Another day, another time, they might be free, but as each day dawned they could see no hope of freedom. There was no relief from the thought of extermination by night, pervasive black ruminations continued, never lit by any glimmer of hope; no candle flickered in their dark despondency, and no ray of sunshine brightened their misery and dejection by day. Even when asleep, through physical and mental exhaustion their brains produced no waves to give them restorative sleep.

The ferocity and frequency of the floggings forced their adaptation towards instinctive reflexes. Their souls were battered into submission by the onslaught and struggled to stay with them, knowing that if they left they were doomed to extinction. The flames of their hearts dwindled into embers, cast into the sky to blow on the wind; a black pall hung over the site blocking out any enlightenment from the heavens.

Over the horizon ordinary people went about their lives, a considerable number with no knowledge of the abhorrent deeds inflicted in this abattoir, and if they did were powerless to do anything about it.

What was the mindset of the men and a few women who abused and murdered millions of children, women and men in the killing camps? The SS showed obedience and conformity with their peers when ordered to kill a human being by an authority figure, and distanced themselves mentally from the victim – were they human beings? The chain of authority started at Hitler who set their minds.

Flying past the plume of the ash of life, which tracked across their flight path, the swan's ancestors routed north on a dogleg to avoid the polluting cloud of carbon drifting across their course, ensuring their virginal feathers remained pristine and they did not lose their breath. The ash fell in the countryside among trees and flowers, covering them as they followed the sun, the breeze shaking it off their petals and returning it to earth from whence it came.

Swans migrating to the Arctic fly across vast areas of earth covered by tundra, essential for their survival, and on towards their preordained destination, the land of the midnight sun. In years to come, when they land, they may find the permafrost is not permanent. They travel towards the land of the Native American Indian, who believes that the Aurora comes to take away the spirits of their dead and animals in an integrated faith in nature. NOTE 48/49

A flight comes in low over the cemetery in formation, and banks and turns to lose height. They trim their wings and glide to land on the lake, their angled up, webbed feet skimming the surface to bring them to a halt. As they swim, barbed wire winds round one of their necks, blood staining its white feathers; they pass some reeds with a fishing line twisted round them. In the past one had a line coiled around its neck, one became ill after swallowing a lump of lead, one had a hook caught in its throat, and one cut its foot on a can lid. NOTE 50

Sometimes, acid black smuts rain down on their spotless purity, and turn leaves from green to brown. In a nearby forest the strident whine of a chainsaw disturbs the silence at the edge of an open area of trees, and a monument to nature crashes down. It damages the branches of trees and kills surrounding flora and fauna, another depletion of the army that takes in carbon dioxide and puts out oxygen, vital to the equilibrium of the global climate. NOTE 51

The swans swim off gracefully towards the red glow, their silhouettes icons of noble beauty against the danger signal of the rising sun, the standard of a nation that adopted a symbol of nature that created and keeps us alive. NOTE 52 During WWII the armed forces of this land committed despicable deeds and atrocities against humanity in the name of an emperor and his desire for power. They take off and fly towards Russia, the red sky in the morning the peoples warning of human rights abuse of any dissidents against the system. NOTE 53

During the Vietnam War – a war between two opposing political systems, the Communist North Vietnamese and the Democratic Government of the USA – fields ran red with the blood of hundreds of thousands when a dictator imposed his dictates by force of arms, and the skulls of the dead were paraded on shelves like wares to be sold. NOTE 54 After Agent Orange was dropped by US planes defoliating trees and making them barren, the Viet Cong army had no cover to disguise their presence, and dug tunnels like animals creating underground villages. It caused genetic mutations and cancer in later life in those exposed to it. The iconic picture of a screaming child running down a road stripped of her skin by napalm, when the burning fluid exploded near her, is an everlasting memory of this war. After years of bombing, which did not deter the Viet Cong and did not win the war, and tens of thousands of US casualties, the US population and soldiers became disillusioned with this 'cold war proxy war'. Eventually the troops left, many with post-traumatic stress, having fought a war of attrition that they could see no reason for; only that the politicians had ordered it: the politicians achieved nothing. Now, in previous war zones, children run and hide in the grass so that they are out of view of their friends, just as the mine underfoot blows off their legs.

On your flanks and rear lie the massed phalanxes of hedged solidarity, square shouldered and trim, to prevent you being caught unawares. All who come to inspect you have to look you in the eye; you see their reactions according to age and whether they are related to you. The middle-aged look earnest and respectful, teenage boys wander uninterested and bored, wishing they were at home playing strategic killing games, and girls wonder why men create so much carnage and unhappiness in the world. Distraught relatives cannot see your inner pain and tears, but you see them on bended knees, a finger gently following their message of love on your chests. Their tears drip into blooms making nectar for droning bees to carry from flower to flower, spreading the message of grief. NOTE 55

Roses, your constant companions in death, march in front and behind you, their crowns of thorns keeping aggressors away. They are in the bloom of youth, and will stay with you at the memorial for some time. Their sweet scents scatters perfume at your feet to disguise the stench of death and purify your souls; from them the colours of your regiments flutter gently in the breeze. The smoke and smell of cordite no longer assails your nostrils, and the noise of screaming salvos is stifled forever; engraved on your hearts are the messages from your loved ones, who will always remember, and march with you into eternity. The sun paints the sky a volcanic red and is bisected by the horizon as the spinning Earth moves it down its final arc for the day.

The creatures of the night fled from the barren desert of desolation, their survival systems obliterated by manmade leviathans moving on metal tracks, which made parallel compression lines on their habitats, crushing all life out of them. The turning forces exerted by these monsters sheared away their homes on Mother Earth. The owl no longer swooped down on the mouse using its unblinking, forward facing, fixed eyes of eternal wisdom. These were compensated by stereoscopic vision, which gave depth of perception, its ability to rotate its neck through 270 degrees, and its asymmetric set ears to increase its capability to localise prey using sound location. Bats no longer flew about avoiding obstacles in their path, catching food using flight directional control. The landscape was ravaged, trees buried and charred, looking like stick insects, and most life exterminated by the battles. It took some time for the recovery in the ecosystems, and when it came, it came slowly, beginning at the bottom of the food chain.

In a nearby field a mouse feverishly forages for food, rustling through the straight lines of erect grain drilled into the ground parallel to your gravestones, his mate squeaking timorously at his tail; his family had been some of the favoured few that had escaped. Overhead, a hawk hovers trying to locate the mice from the noise of the moving crop; it dips a wing, banks, and loses height, hovering for a short time before diving onto its prey.

Chapter 9

Here lies a mariner, RN, the initials of his branch of the armed forces anchored to his chest, who was confined by the fires of hell and sank past Poseidon into the depths before coming to his final resting place; a watery grave entombed in a gun turret, his visible memory set in stone shoulder to shoulder with his comrades. NOTE 56

His ship, a heavy cruiser that was more manoeuvrable but less heavily armed and less armour plated than the enemy ship, was bearing down at an angle of 30 degrees astern. The captain wanted to fire a broadside before it got out of range, and ordered a turn to a parallel course, exposing the ship to enemy fire before her guns could be brought to bear.

In a rear gun turret he peered out through a slit in his flash proof clothes. Shells and propellant came up separately from the magazine on a hoist; a mechanical interlock ensured that there was never an open portal from the gun house to the magazine down which an explosive ignition might pass. Flash tight doors opened and closed to allow the passage of shells and cordite into the turret. A shell was tipped into the breech and propellant brought forward behind it, which was rammed home with a hydraulic ram. The guns were ready to fire: he waited for the ranging instructions to lay them.

In the Director's Control Room, the angle of elevation was calculated using an opto-electro-mechanical computational ranging system; an analogue computer that fed into a Fire Control Table. Trigonometric data derived from ship and enemy speed, distance, course and convergence were factored into an equation. Pitch, roll, wind speed, humidity, Coriolis effect, powder mixture, and other parameters were taken into account to give the firing solution.

In the distance the German ship fired a ranging salvo, which straddled his ship, a fountain of water splashing on the deck. The angle of elevation of the next salvo was correctly adjusted, and following its predetermined trajectory found its range. A funnel collapsed onto the deck killing men and starting fires. The next shell hit amidships, a storm of shrapnel levelling many, followed by a direct hit on a forward turret. The members of the medical team left alive tended to the men as best they could, but many would die. Packing staunched the bleeding from their wounds; injections of morphine were given to make them comfortable.

A sister ship raced between the two laying a smoke screen, a huge wake of water arcing from the stern as the engines were pushed to maximum revolutions. The captain ordered a change of course, knowing that he would not be able to use his remaining guns effectively, but wanting to take damage limitation measures. Although the fire control centre was damaged, the sailor's turret kept firing; the next shell landed near it and started a fire. His conduct was exemplary ensuring that his shipmates escaped first. The blistering heat burned the crew's exposed areas, smoke choking and blinding them: a wall of fire trapped him.

The next armour-piercing salvo landed on the other forward gun turret; the explosion descended the elevator shaft striking a direct blow to the magazine. A chain reaction multiplied the energy several thousand-fold and it exploded in the bowels of the ship lifting the deck, leaving a ragged hole belching flames, and a massive breach in the hull below the water line, an invitation that the ever-ready sea accepted, the law of displacement of water being negated; the ship's fate became obvious and the captain ordered, 'abandon ship'.

Scores of men jumped into the freezing water, but because the ship went down so quickly few rescue rafts had been thrown over the side, and they struggled to reach them through lakes of burning oil. Some were unconscious, their faces stripped of skin, a black crust replacing it. Their shipmates, who were not injured, tried to pull them towards the rafts, but it was a struggle through the swell and conflagration. The captain remained on the bridge until all the crew had left. A frigate bird soared on the thermals from the inferno on the sinking man of war.

The captain of an enemy ship that attacked convoys held to a code of honour early in the war. If there were no other enemy ships involved in the battle, or if it was a merchant ship, he could make the decision to pick up survivors; it could have been his own men in the same position. He was in the German Navy, not in the Gestapo, SS. or a member of the Nazi party, and able to make up his own mind about rescuing British sailors, although he faced the possibility of being tried for treason. Rescued sailors were made as comfortable as possible; the ship's medical team treated the injured. However, after a U-boat sank the Laconia, subsequent events lead to a Standard Operating Procedure order being made prohibiting this. NOTE 57

Brave men sailed on a sea at the top of the world in the Arctic convoys to Archangel and Murmansk. They carried weapons of war to a Communist country known for its human rights abuse, arming it in its fight against Fascism. They endured atrocious weather conditions with constant freezing temperatures, pounding waves, and constant threat of attack by planes and submarines – if a ship was sunk no one survived. The sailors had to hammer ice off the ship's superstructures to prevent them capsizing, and risked being thrown overboard. Few people heard about them; no one knew what they did for the war; no one knew about their sacrifice. They have belatedly been awarded a medal, the Arctic Star, for their courage.

> We walk alone yet together,
> Soul in soul you and me,
> The sea lapping at our feet.
> This life we live in moves on,
> But we are never apart.

> The sun framed by clouds kisses
> The portrait of the evening sea.
> A wave of warmth comes to meet us,
> And gives me the strength to go on,
> Until we are at rest together.

> This cruel world goes on transforming,
> God's creatures keep rearranging,
> Forever – for this is how we all became.

A EULOGY TO ABSENT FRIENDS

> As I walk I feel your hand,
> Yet there is only one set of footprints in the sand.
> The sea flows to its tidal reach,
> And ebbs to leave a flat, smooth beach.

His brother, who was too young to go to war, worked in the Post Office. Official telegrams from the War Department informing relatives of the loss of a loved one were received there, and delivered by a Military Chaplin, or by him on his bike – he was called 'an angel of death'. It had a standard format; 'I regret to inform you that your son was killed - - - or, reported missing in action - - - '. A letter of sympathy from the soldier's company officer accompanied it. Everyone dreaded the telegram: some never sent one for the rest of their lives.

With many parents away from home, or working long hours outside home, older children were often left to look after themselves during the day. They played games in fields, or in their streets, which involved friendly interaction between individual females and males, and mixed teams. They helped clear up after air raids and ran errands to the corner shop for the elderly. Grandparents and neighbours helped look after younger children. When a neighbour's house was bombed the residents were offered a bed, food, and lent clothes and furniture, and when someone was reported dead the relatives received ongoing support from friends and neighbours, not just next door, but farther up the street. They all waited for the telegram: it could be their loved one – in some communities half the men were killed.

The Women's Royal Naval Service was disbanded after WWI but re-founded to allow the men to work for the fleet. Initially the work was limited to clerical, driving and domestic work, but later their responsibilities included operating radar and communications equipment; some naval stations had all female anti-aircraft teams, although females were not allowed to fire the guns initially, only fuse the shells.

The Naval Censorship Branch drafted women to Bletchley Park where they supported the work of the Enigma code breakers. Women generally found men hostile to their presence, but once they saw they were making a positive contribution to the war effort they became more amiable.

The manpower shortage allowed them to crew harbour launches, picking up people on landing craft anchored at sea. They carried out mine spotting and loaded torpedoes onto submarines. They trained as welders and carpenters, repairing ships in naval bases. On D-Day, they piloted small craft across to France, and towed disabled vessels back to port for repairs often carried out by WRNS mechanics.

A butterfly, Red Admiral of the fleet, settles on your shoulder, opening and closing its wings to warm them, and its body to enable it to feed. It flaps its wings and flies away, but enticed by a whim and ambivalence, it creates a cycle of positive feedback by shifting course and doubling back, a decision that might change the destiny of the world. NOTE 58

The Monarch of the world of butterflies, the king of navigators of the insect world, visits the cemetery on its 2,000mile odyssey to rest and replenish its energy reserves. The number that makes it this far is decreasing each year due to deforestation and climate change; here there are no chemical fertilizers and no insecticides on plants.

A white dove on its migration path over the parade heard the pleas for peace emanating from your anguished souls. She flew down and landed on one of your shoulders, cooing commiserations to you in your despair. She had lost a mate, who was killed when he was perching in a tree near to where a shell landed, and although she had found another, he was never forgotten. She always stopped on her yearly journey to pay her respects to your respective souls.

> Here, beneath the shadow of a willow aslant, creaking gently in its old age, weeping with rage and frustration at men's futility, lies a solitary member of the fair sex segregated in death; the sun never to bless her maiden face again. NOTE 59 She was the saviour of the emotions (SOE) of the emotionally bereft but has no honours on her chest. NOTE 60 She had not known love of the heart, only love of the mind; her work was her love and fellow human beings in this brutal episode in history, and she received deliverance. Her tenderness and kindness showed when you talked to her about dying and never seeing those at home again; she hid her emotions until she was by herself. She showed compassion to you, and wanted you to know that someone cared deeply in your last moments; it was a comfort in place of your loved ones. No one could understand or appreciate that happiness was ordinary everyday life, unless one had experienced sadness.

The enemy transferred a captured, wounded, high-ranking British officer behind their lines; it was decided that a rescue mission be sent. She volunteered to go with the medical team that accompanied the soldiers, but stopped a few miles from the enemy positions. The mission was accomplished, but they were ambushed when returning; she fell, mortally wounded. The group had orders to leave the wounded because the return of the officer was of paramount importance to security.

Left with four soldiers who were dead or dying, her life flashed before her. She remembered what men had said so often to her, how the important things in life are only appreciated when it is about to end. A young man, who had fallen nearby, stretched out to touch her and asked if she was afraid to die; death had looked her in the face so often, it was neither friend nor foe. She remembered men's faces, how she had been with them at the end to make them feel loved. Alone in a frozen field with no one to share her feelings, she found strength in the thought she had consoled others in their torment; she was not alone and never would be. She had given the most important thing in life to those souls when they departed, and they would carry it with them forever to sustain them in their search for their loved ones. She had given the ultimate gift, the gift of her spirit, a legacy of love and mental strength that would remain with those to whom she gave solace, who survived when she passed on. They would hold the memory of her sensitivity and cherish her kind words.

The last energy from her touch flowed; her comrade slipped into oblivion and lay silent, but her soul pulsated with the dynamic source and started its transmigration into peace in the afterlife. The fundamental force in good was with her and did not let her falter in her flight. She died in peace knowing that she had gained spiritually in her short life.

> Soothing your brows,
> With the tips of her care,
> She calmed your fears,
> With a healing refrain.
>
> Wiping your tears,
> With a sigh of a breath,
> She lifted your sadness,
> With a gentle smile,
>
> She clung on to hope,
> That might have been lost,
> Searching for a faith,
> That was so hard to find.
>
> Blowing away doubts,
> On a caress of the breeze,
> She allayed a dread,
> That might never occur.
>
> Grasping at thoughts,
> That slipped through your fingers,
> She gave a hand,
> That was never withdrawn.
>
> She embraced a love,
> That came from the soul,
> Guiding your spirits,
> To eternal rest.

J. N. SLATER

Walking her will
Through your depths of despair,
She carried the weight,
Of your whole world.

Clutching at dreams,
That blew in the wind,
She held to the truth,
In her hurting heart.

She held a moment,
That gave life meaning,
Seizing a chance,
That went without saying.

Kissing the stars,
That appeared in the night,
She welcomed the dawn,
That gave her respite.

Carrying the light,
That led out of darkness,
She decided the way,
And where to go forward.

She searched for peace,
In the heart of mankind,
Seeking a sign,
That the war would soon end.

She made a white poppy,
Which complimented a red.
A symbol for peace,
And an end to all wars.

> She opened the door
> That led out to peace,
> Drawing a fine line,
> Never to be crossed,
> Underlining –<u>The End,</u>
> That was for all time.

At one end of the spectrum women were used as secret agents; they were members of the SOE (Special Operations Executive). In 1944 they were parachuted into France to find information to support the Allies landings. It was exceptionally dangerous; some were captured, tortured in horrific ways, and murdered by the Gestapo – the evil arm of the Nazi killing machine. A memorial has just been built to honour these brave women of the SOE.

At the other end of the spectrum some women became entertainers. Singers, especially, brought happiness with their optimistic songs of peace; the spirits of everyone at home were boosted.

When storm clouds blow over the parade ground the anger of the gods reverberates down through the centuries, striking a thunderous note that can be heard rumbling around the valley, and echoing off the surrounding hills. Potential forces of energy accumulate within them, the same forces that powered you and created emotion and memory, and the infernal legions strike your gravestones with bolts of light.

This energy – lightning – forms when ice balls hail down stripping electrons from ice crystals lower down in clouds, setting up a negative polarity between clouds and the atmosphere, and between clouds and the ground. An electrical potential builds, and a lightning discharge occurs when the distribution of positive and negative charges form a sufficiently strong electric field, resulting in the release of an immense amount of electromagnetic energy, lighting up the sky, and creating shock, heat and radio waves when the potential is temporarily discharged to Earth.

NOTE 61 The lightning discharges produce nitrates that fall to Earth in rain as fertiliser, and ozone to protect us from the sun – our master in the sky – for that which made us can destroy us.

> The wrath, unleashed in a stream of crackling light, wounded a nearby tree, blasting off a large branch even though it survived the battles. It tracked to Mother Earth leaving a scar like a bandolier on the uniform of one of you, cutting through the message on your chest, and abbreviating it. The headstone was removed and replaced with a replica, your epitaph carved so that you carry it with pride once more. At times it has set alight the dry grass in the nearby forests, the fire burning gently, meandering through tall pine trees, scorching them but not setting them alight, and clearing the earth of debris for a new generation of flora.

Chapter 10

Towards the end of the war, some of humanity faced the spectre of nuclear energy released from uranium produced in a thermo-nuclear pile, which was transmuted into an incandescent blinding fireball, 'like the sun rising out of the earth and exploding'; it generated a massive blast, hot wind and a firestorm. This maelstrom of malevolence mushroomed over an immense depression on a landscape of devastation, lit by a sky of flickering tongues of fire, surrounded by a sea of lifeless decay with not one nanosecond of half-life left. The apparition of the Fifth horseman of the Apocalypse, his skull cloaked in black, sat astride his rising grey mount, a gamma radiation cloud of unspeakable depravity; the ash disturbed by his horse's feet shrouded everything. The dreaded miasma spread its invisible plague; blown on winds it travelled long distances permeating every nook and cranny. It annihilated souls by the thousands, stripping electrons off atoms and molecules, upsetting the symmetry of charge, and forming free radicals that damaged D.N.A. and the ability of cells to grow and replicate; a mortal wound to the body tissues.

Wind blew dust through a deserted dump of radioactive waste in a time warped by lifelessness, and carried it through the deserted streets of a flattened ghost town, over crossroads, filling the shells of derelict houses with the debris of time. This dust, laden with the molecules of life, blotted out the sun making a 'nuclear winter': the sun would not deign to light the day on man's last futile game.

The day started beautiful, children chatting on their way to school, aware of planes that flew overhead, in their innocence wondering why Japan was being attacked by America. The initial lateral flash depleted the massed armies of trees; their fire breaks traversed in a trice, leaving stunted black dwarves. Chill gales blew for an aeon forming icicles at degrees to the vertical on their branches. Their skeletons waved their arms about in a sterile wilderness, trying to attract attention in a barren desert where no life form could see their gesticulations.

The initial gamma ray burst caused acute death. Bodies near the hypocentre evaporated due to the heat; there were pale areas on stone where people had existed, and then been vaporised. Some were cremated to cinders; they disintegrated on their funeral pyres, their organs and tissues carbonised. Coins that had been in their pockets fused; a trail of change from the local shop. Beside them lay soft metal fused into nightmare surrealistic sculptures, blobs hanging from them like decorations. Farther from the hypocentre charred bodies forlornly tried to touch their loved ones, still showing respect for each other; a boy was frozen in his last act like a tree in a petrified forest, his arms fused to his chest in prayer. The smell of incineration hung in the air from bodies fried in the conflagration, stripped of their skin like a side of beef – no one existed to smell it. Fish in a metal container was burned to a cinder; beside it laid the skeletons of a dog and its owner. The leaves of a tree were toasted: a bird sitting in it roasted. A lady saw the sun explode at two thousand feet: she burned: she fell: our star was still present in the sky.

Farther away the flash branded exposed skin; clothes were protective. White clothes reflected UV light; black clothes absorbed heat, charred, and caught fire. The patterns on their clothes were duplicated by the patterns on their skin; a man's braces left protective diagonal lines on his back. An old woman with a hat on, who was facing the flash, suffered no burns; she was bent forward, hands together in respect, greeting a friend at the point of detonation. An old man, who was sitting enjoying the early morning sun beside a shrub with large leaves, was left with a pattern of one of them on his face where it was protected from the heat. A flash burn the shape of a car was left on the flank of a horse that was standing behind it. Radioactive black rain fell on people who were dehydrated; they opened their mouths and the Black Death dripped in. A river full of bodies flowed through the inferno towards the sea, and a communal watery grave.

Partially damaged buildings cast permanent shadows on nearby buildings they sheltered from the blast – the mark of Satan. Roads running across the flattened city, bereft of any houses, made a crosshatch appearance on the landscape. Buses and cars were blown over and deposited metres away. In one direction all that was left was a Shinto shrine, the arch made of elements that withstood the blast, and round pillars that allowed the blast to go round it, the smooth stone etched by fine stone debris. In another direction two religious deities made of metal and still intact leaned forwards towards each other in a posture of respect.

A watch stopped at 8.15 in the morning lay on the floor of a building, the end of its duration of timekeeping, and the beginning of humankind's countdown in its search for the means of extermination of our race.

A young child, who had been sheltered from the blast, sat on the ground crying surrounded by devastation; she had been protected by the flash and blast by part of a stronger building. She saw her mother, father, and sister scorched; she would have to wait for help, if any came in time. A man stumbled along carrying an eye in one hand, and his other burned hand covering his face and fused eyelids. He got down on his knees and prayed to his deity for release from his agony. Fire raged through wooden structures; flames blew from a fractured gas pipe adding to the Dantesque inferno. A naked baby, who was crawling, was seared on its bottom and thrown into its flattened house. A man, who was smoking at the corner of a sturdy building, had his nose and mouth singed, and his cigarette turned to ash: around him for 400 metres all the buildings were razed to the ground. A mother, hanging out her washing, saw the contrails of a single American bomber streaming across the sky; her body was protected from the flash by a white sheet. A man lay at the rear of a car, which had been torched by the flash and stripped of its paint; its boot had been opened by the blast. It contained a smouldering suitcase waiting to be claimed; the occupants were going to visit relations. Both car doors were open and the windows blown out; the occupants lay in front of the car, scalped when their heads hit the windscreen frame when they exited it. Beside the car lay a mangled bicycle, both machines never to move again. A bus was blown onto its side, the passengers' combusted in the sitting position before the blast hit them. A queue standing beside the bus was incinerated, caught mid-sentence with their mouths open talking about the war and their honourable Emperor, their skeletons piles of bones gathered against the underside of the bus whose wheels were naked – it would never cross the city again. The coins for their fares lay fused, gleaming in the rubble, a glimmer of light for humanity in the darkness.

Bald, wild-eyed mothers stumbled and crawled, begging for help. Some were blind, eyelids fused by the flash, with black, ulcerated flesh and skin hanging down; they were unable to vocalise their pain. They pathetically carried their babies without realising they were dead. Some had children trapped under the rubble, powerless to save them they had to make the impossible choice whether to leave, or die with them. They would have to live with this decision for the rest of their lives. A baby, and her mother from whom she was feeding, had their faces charred on one side; the mother's chest was left with a burn the outline of the baby's head. A woman ran along a street, the clothes on her back on fire; they burned through and the front fell off.

Birds sang: then silence. Large trees were uprooted and thrown a distance away, and the leaves of trees not affected by the blast turned autumn colours due to radiation. A man's head lay on the ground, his teeth showing between his charred lips, his scalp bald, and black holes where the flash had burned out his eyes. Hurricane force winds blew chunks of stone and metal into people, ripping apart their bodies. The blast produced a pressure wave that caused air embolism, haemorrhaging into internal cavities, and tore muscle off bone.

Some, who lived a distance from the centre of the blast, were saved because they lived in an earthquake resistant building; the structure was not completely flattened. The flash permanently blinded some, the same as if they looked at the sun for too long.

Those surviving injury, but affected by radiation, suffered hair loss, vomiting and shivering, followed in days by disorientation, coma, and death from the direct effect of radiation on the brain. The less severely affected bled from body orifices resulting in anaemia and weakness, overwhelming infection due to lack of white cells, diarrhoea and dehydration; they died a death by torture. In the ensuing years many died from cancer, and there was a trans-generational risk of genetic damage. Dropping a nuclear bomb is genocide; genocide that carries on for years. We use the energy of the sun and take elements from Earth to build us: men use them to destroy us – we return them when we die.

High above the cemetery, a lonely eagle soars in spirals on thermals from the warm ground. A shell blast killed her mate when he flew from their eerie containing a precious egg, seeking sanctuary in a rocky crevice. Above the eagle, planes that are descendants of the ones that attacked you, their watery signature of twin contrails cross hatching the sky, fly at different altitudes carrying travellers to their holidays in warm climes. They greedily guzzle tons of fuel, their engine emissions spraying out greenhouse gases and the water of life, forming cirrus clouds that block the heat of the sun, but also the reflection of heat back into space; the net result an increase in atmospheric temperature.

The travellers may find the evidence of man's ravages on nature, but not necessarily understand or care.

They will sit in nature and be ravaged by it, accelerated by man's ravages on nature. They are out of reach of your tormented souls, insulated from the cold they talk about sun and relaxation. Their worries are if the flight will be late, if the weather will be good, and if the accommodation will be suitable: few have visited the Stygian darkness of a foxhole. NOTE 62

Some travel to see the remains of buildings built by the Greek and Roman civilisations, which brought beauty, culture, advancement, and the beginnings of our legal system. They slaughtered human beings by the hundreds of thousands to obtain power and prosperity, at the cost of death and destruction.

A woman, widowed by war, walks up a winding path on a hill above the parade, heather and tussocks of grass surround her, tinting the hillside a blush of purple. In the distance sheep graze in a field, giving a green and white polka dot pattern, and around the perimeter there is a dilapidated dry stonewall.

She comes across a hide where empty shotgun cartridges had been scattered on the ground, ammunition used in the unilateral attack on birds by humans after their declaration of war. She climbs past a rocky outcrop adorned with alpine flowers clinging to rocky crevices. At the summit on her left stands a single wind turbine, and on her right six, silent sentinels surveying the valley.

Due to lack of wind, important as a renewable energy source, the turbines were not creating electricity. The Earth's supply of fossil fuel to produce electricity will eventually run out if we do not annihilate each other before then – and what will we have achieved? Our civilization will die long before the Earth dies, scorched by our sun. Will we live long enough to invent an interstellar propulsion system to make the journey to the nearest planet to see if there is life and compare our civilisations? And if we do, what do we do when we get there – integrate into their society? NOTE 63 International societies on Earth cannot integrate. Would they want to share food when their food supply might have become unstable, they were living a subsistence existence, and the population might have reached a critical level due to the inhabitants living longer? Wars might be being fought to gain agricultural land. Our goal must be to try to make peace throughout our world before we can ever consider ourselves fit to serve as ambassadors for our Earth. NOTE 64

A mist that hangs over the summit clears as she reaches it when a blustery breeze blows it away. Tousling her hair, it veers from north to north-northwest, starts the turbines, and funnels down a valley scattered with grey, granite rocks gleaming in sun. She takes a bearing on the cemetery and heads off down the valley.

Wending her way she walks on an old road, which had been used by horse-drawn carts, and follows the course of a stream, crossing a narrow hump back bridge, which had been marched on by soldiers in the past; high up on the valley side are the remains of an old redoubt. She reaches a brook bubbling and babbling over boulders that had been smoothed by water over millennia, sits down on a patch of grass on which she used to have a picnic with her husband, and drinks water from a crystal clear stream. NOTE 65

Her husband had died defending his country, but his body had never been found. The nearest she could get to him was to visit the cemetery where his comrades were buried. She talked to them saying how much she missed them all, and what she was doing in her life – we speak to know we are not alone ('A la recherché du temps perdu'). NOTE 66 She told them that despite their sacrifice peace on Earth had not been achieved; a horrific weapon had been developed that could eradicate all forms of life. Peace and tranquillity prevailed: she questioned the meaning and purpose of existence.

Since her husband's death she had ploughed her own philosophy of life and went out of her way to help others; she gave a monologue to the men who listened attentively. Some of us walk a pedestrian pathway through life, taking right-angled turns that end in cul-de-sacs. We don't understand our reasons, and the decisions we make and why; in an attempt to come to a conclusion we take two steps forward and then one to the side. NOTE 67 Some of us take a perilous route; we live on the edge, never knowing if we are going to fall, but believing we will not. Some of us pass others in distress like ships in the night, never caring or thinking about stopping to throw them a lifeline when they are cast onto the rocks, wanting to reach our destination as fast as possible, not wanting to carry more of a burden than we think we have, and not intending to increase it.

On our journey some of us take a direct course showing kindness to others and receiving in return – for it is as much of a gift to receive, as it is to give. We smooth the way for others who are less well-off due to infirmity or in anguish, and help those who take a tortuous, serpentine path of emotional unavailability. They lack empathy and are disengaged, not being in touch with, or unable to externalise their feelings. They do not want to get too close to others and wall themselves off; the walls need to be broken down so that their souls can rise from the rubble and their emotions become available. She held to the tenet that happiness is a lack of sadness, and exaltation could not be held for long before a plummet back to normal everyday life.

In the distance a mountain rises with its snow-white wig in winter, and its bald patch and purple garland of heather in summer; it had watched the devastation and the inevitable end. Its face, battered by the elements, has been left pockmarked by heavy artillery shells. Its skirt of pines has been felled, leaving it denuded, the earth below eroded away by wind and rain. Its two corries look like orbits, deep and dark in summer, and white and sparkling in winter. Their tarns brim over with tears at humankind's futility, and run down its face, feeding into a waterfall that sparkles in the sun. Scree, growing larger every year, tumbles down its front like a dark beard, evidence of man's crumbling existence.

Wind deflected upwards by the mountain gives lift beneath the wings of an eagle that soars over its chest. It blows clouds that have formed by air picking up water over the sea, which caress the top of the mountain, and swirl on the lee side, depositing rain on the land. When the wind abates, and clouds clear, the sun creates thermals that lift the eagle to lofty heights. Sometimes it is gentle and loving, wafting cool breezes, sometimes brusque and irritable, snapping at plants and trees, and sometimes it roars in anger.

At the end of the valley, on the plain near the shore, lies an oblong concrete structure with two waisted chimneys belching out steam – a nuclear power plant run on an element that provides us with energy, but able to destroy us.

A viaduct spans the valley, its majestic arches the same design as the aqueducts that the Romans built to carry water. A few of these structures still exist, and some have two tiers of arches, monuments to their advanced civilisation. During the Industrial Revolution they were built to carry steam trains, they now carry trains that use cleaner forms of energy.

Below the viaduct runs a river meandering towards the sea, its course changing over millennia by rubbing its shoulders against its banks. At the source the river is a dribble, then a stream, gathering momentum until it widens and slows. Its sisters pay tribute and join it feeding its estuary, which pours forth infinite wisdom and knowledge from its mouth. Its children, distributaries, spawn from it spreading youthful hope into the sea. One head of the river falls off the mountain into a chasm, becoming a raging torrent, and spume blows on the wind when the water drops vertically forming a rainbow, the visible spectrum of light. The volume of its voice swells in shallows and is quiet when the water runs deep. It embraces rocks in its path when it breaks over them, and massages them with its supple fingers, leaving eddies and goodbye kisses.

It has passed for aeons and will carry on for millions of years, returning on its endless journey. It leaves its mother's arms and flows to its mouth, evaporates from the sea to its bearer, the wind, and is blown back over the land to its source and rebirth.

There is an old mill by the river. Water powers the wheel and through a series of cogs a stone is turned, grinding cereal to make flour. Man may harness the power of water but he will never contain it.

The sinking sun sets on a fiery sky, casting a shadow from the spire of the village church, which creeps across the cemetery for residents who had died naturally, but also through war, the point of the spire dividing the cemetery in two. In the weekly service the residents of the village give thanks for your sacrifice, and their freedom from tyranny.

The pink hue of the contrails of a plane that has changed course by 30 degrees makes an optimistic tick in the sky on humankind's checklist of things that have to be done to save our race, until a smear of shades of grey temporarily obscures the sun. The storm clouds of war roll relentlessly onwards in the distance.

Many an ancient warrior has led himself through this verdant pasture, by the quiet waters in front of the cross, to inspect the parade. They walk alone through this epitome of man's inhumanity to man with their thoughts of battles long ago. They remember your faces when a joke was cracked at a fellow warrior's expense, a forced laugh changing your nervous, gloomy demeanour for a short while. They understand the anguish of your souls, without invitation it has visited them so often in the past; they have tried to shut it out but they know they will take it to the grave.

One stands before you recognising the names of fallen friends, with the sure and certain knowledge that he would be reunited with you when he died. He had seen you fall, heard your souls escape with a mournful wail, tears coming to his eyes as he remembers the noise of battle compared to the quiet of the parade. His grief extended to home where a mate had been killed by a bomber dropping its load of bombs onto her home.

Here, crest on his chest, marches a soul unknown except to all his family who dearly miss him, his dog tag separated from him when he fell. Many had fallen and lost their identity when they were buried, Mother Earth embracing her sons once again. At one with her, your souls left to ascend to a higher plane, knowing they would intercept the roaming spirits of your loved ones searching for you. It is a hard task, but they keep searching, forever hopeful, knowing you have not laid down your life in vain.

> Through the mist,
> Across the lake,
> A skirling noise was heard,
> It brought a swell of pride,
> When you were about to gird.

> In the thrill of anticipation,
> For the battle soon to come,
> It filled your souls with courage,
> And your spirits were set free.

Can we change the course of history, make peace in humanity and prevent men sacrificing themselves in a 'just war' for the greater good? And how do we do this? If we solve the mysteries of the universe, the nature of reality, where we come from, and how we got here, can we not stop the reality of war? Could there be a parallel universe where life exits, and peace reigns? We are an infinitesimal blip on the space-time continuum, and cannot go back to reverse our history, but it does not mean that the massacre must go on.

Would inhabitants of another planet warmly welcome us if we arrive carrying weapons, or launch a pre-emptive strike? Are we naïve enough to think they would be different to us? Their evolutionary history would be the same. Men would have killed animals for millennia to enable the family to survive, and each other to defend their land. If they were at the same stage of evolution they would be fighting for power over other countries. NOTE 68 Why would we want to visit another planet if we thought they might harm us? We need the threat of retaliation to try to keep peace on Earth, but if the threat turns into reality we might destroy ourselves with the ultimate weapon. Are we more advanced than the civilisations that worshipped sun gods, and carried out ritual sacrifices in their name? Could social networking between young people of different nations stop the spectre of war by sharing friendship?

What conventions, rules of engagement, and niceties of killing can exist in war when there are no rules in peace? The course of history was changed by the assassination of a president who wanted to end racial discrimination of black people, including men who fought for the United States in World War II, and bring some measure of peace to the world. Might the world have been a better place sooner had he not been assassinated? Now, fanatical terrorists kill using suicide bombs and planes. NOTE 69

Can there ever be peace unless women are involved 50 percent in the decision making process to keep the status quo? They would not want their children, relatives, and innocent civilians killed; they would want to communicate, conciliate, compromise, and mediate. We insulate ourselves from the horrors of men's violence in distant countries where fellow men are powerless to intervene without causing more bloodshed. Should we not be trying to prevent the violence arising in the first place? But how, when it has been in humanity's nature for so long? Future generations will observe the history, but will the men who start these wars inspect the parade grounds of the lost; will their consciences be tormented by the souls who are butchered in the name of power and greed?

You march in peace and at rest with your companions who have given their lives for the cause so that we may live. When will the massacre end; when will friendship, peace, and tranquillity prevail in the world as it does in this revered ground?

The thunder of the storm has left, the fires of hell doused by rain for a short time, but is this a lull before the next? Your souls will not rest in peace until the violence has ended, releasing them from their endless journey, and returning to be with you in Mother Earth.

> To be so very far away, and yet to be so near,
> Means that your memory is always kept alive.
> To live within the hearts of those who dearly love you,
> Means that your memory will never die.

J. N. SLATER

EPITAPH

As in the beginning there was the end,
So in the end there was the beginning.
As you came in advance,
So they went in retreat.
As there was chaos in action,
So there is order at rest.
As in life you were opposed,
So in death you are joined.
As in battle you were many,
So in death you are one.
As in your life there was death,
So in your death there is life.
As in your life there was sadness,
So in our sadness there is peace.

Notes

Page 4
NOTE 1
Insane that madness – hyperbole.

Page 20
NOTE 2
In adversity aspiring for the stars – 'Per ardua ad astra' – through adversity to the stars – the RAF motto. – 'Up the hill to the local cinema' – cinemas on RAF bases are called 'Astra'.

Page 21
NOTE 3
Burning of elements – Alfred Nobel – to atone for his discovery and development of explosives he instituted his award for the promotion of peace.

Page 24
NOTE 4
George – a colloquialism for the invisible co-pilot, an autopilot, in the cockpit.

Page 27
NOTE 5
'Nil bastardo carborundum' – don't let the bastards grind you down.

Page 27
NOTE 6
Native American tipi – a conical shaped tent made of buffalo hide; there was a gap at the top to let smoke escape from a fire.

Page 30
NOTE 7
All types of metal were collected from households for munitions, including essential items that ladies used to make themselves look their best: hair clips, combs, and make up boxes. You can still see the stumps where railings round front gardens were cut off. These were transported to steelworks and melted down to make the tools of war.

Steelworkers were in a reserved occupation needed for making the implements of war. A blackout could not be enforced for steelworks, which were a target for bombers, because the furnaces could not be shut down.

Men were conscripted to work in coalmines, chosen by a ballot for this occupation by Ernest Bevin (a British statesman). They were selected if the last digit of their registration (ID) number matched the number that was pulled out of a hat; coal was needed to stoke the fires of war. Young male teachers joined the forces, but older and less able men took their places, and scientists were involved in research into new materials and developments in war weapons and detection systems.

Page 32
NOTE 8
Overworld c.f. underworld.

Page 33
NOTE 9
Gun cleaning rod – stamen

Page 33
NOTE 10
Recalibrate their magnetic navigation systems. To recalibrate their magnetic navigation systems they use the changing pattern of sunlight, quantum entanglement, exchange of quanta of energy, the photoelectric, electro-molecular (cis to trans change in configuration of the rhodopsin molecule) and the electro-magnetic effect. In response to a triggering voltage change to a neurone, a wave of depolarisation allows sodium and potassium to pass through voltage gated ion channels, creating a proton electrochemical gradient and an action potential to develop, which enables them to 'see' the Earth's magnetic field.

Page 36
NOTE 11
In Lloyds of London the Lutine bell used to be rung once when a ship was sunk.

Page 36
NOTE 12
A thermocline can exist at 400–500 feet but usually start at much greater depths.

Page 37
NOTE 13
'Nodding donkeys' – oil wells that pump crude oil out of the ground.

Page 40
NOTE 14
'raft slapping in the water' – literary licence – he only had a buoyancy aid.

Page 41
NOTE 15
'Rime of the Ancient Mariner' – Coleridge – the mariner killed the albatross – idiom 'an albatross around one's neck'. No cross in penance around their necks – the crew did not show any penance for over-fishing; fishing that is causing a decline in sea bird numbers, which are being caught on hooks used in line fishing.

Page 41
NOTE 16
"Water, water, everywhere, nor any drop to drink'. – 'Rime of the Ancient Mariner'.

Page 41
NOTE 17
'Raptures of the Deep' – 'Livresse des profondeurs' – 'drunkenness of the deep' – nitrogen narcosis. Jacques Cousteau was the inventor of the 'Aqua Lung'. If a diver was only breathing air, when he reached a certain depth, the nitrogen in the air was forced into his brain, causing confusion and hallucinations. In the past, divers have been known to take off their masks and offer them to passing fish.

Page 42
NOTE 18
Dolphins and whales, driven by evolution, swim north to reproduce in the area where the taste and smell of the sea produced by silt from rivers identifies precisely where they should stop. Toxic chemicals, heavy metals, and non-organic debris that do not degrade change the signature of these rivers. The effluent kills plankton and algae, and because they are at the top of the food chain there is less food for fish lower

down the chain. They move north into cooler waters seeking food, resulting in fish stocks diminishing in the wrong season, which affects sea birds feeding locations and reproduction. The irony is that when plankton dies they sink to the ocean floor, and over millions of years the carbon is changed to hydrocarbons (crude oil). Plankton absorbs and scatters light, which warms the topmost layers of the ocean, and produce volatile chemicals, which contribute to cloud formation; both help to keep ocean temperatures down. Through photosynthesis, plankton absorbs carbon dioxide dissolved in the sea.

Human industry has increased CO_2 levels in the atmosphere, resulting in less radiation of heat from the Earth, an increase in air temperature and decreased absorption of CO_2 due to rising sea temperatures. Consequently there is an increased death rate of plankeon, which are not in abundance when needed by birds and animals.

The sea absorbs CO_2 forming carbonic acid; increasing levels in the atmosphere are in some areas of the world killing reefs and leaving them barren (a debatable argument – some authorities say there is a decreased amount of CO_2 absorbed as sea water temperatures increase). Increasing sea temperatures, nitrates (nitrous oxide from agricultural fertiliser is a major cause of warming of the atmosphere), and phosphorus in water run-off from farms into rivers may stimulate the growth of toxic phytoplankton algal blooms, which release poisonous hydrogen sulphide and are harmful to humans and animals. When algae die the decomposition takes O_2 out of the water killing fish, worms and aquatic insects, which sea birds and marine mammals live on. Toxic agricultural and industrial chemicals are occasionally washed into rivers killing fish, eradicating their survival systems and leaving them belly up, the cumulative effect causing D.N.A. mutations in humans and animals.

Death of the Amazon Rainforest due to lower precipitation in this part of the world is releasing increasing amounts of CO_2, causing a positive feedback cycle and growing CO_2 levels; logging decreases the number of trees available to absorb CO_2. CO_2 absorbed by the sea forms carbonic acid that in the arctic is preventing molluscs forming their shells, and killing corals and the fish that live on them. With increasing air and sea temperatures the Polar ice caps may melt, the sea may expand, and there may be wide spread flooding.

Page 43
NOTE 19
King of Fishers – Jesus – allusion to the Christ symbolism inherent in fishing and the miracle of the fish catch.

Page 43
NOTE 20
League – an obsolete measurement of distance that was used by mariners.

Page 43
NOTE 21
Quicksilver – mercury – heavy metal poisoning. Sub-lethal amounts of heavy metals accumulate in fish causing biochemical changes in their cells: humans are at risk through contamination of the food chain.

Page 43
NOTE 22
'Pour oil on troubled water' – the smoothing effect of oil on choppy water due to its surface tension.

Drilling for oil in the Arctic and Antarctic – possibility of oil leaks damaging the environment – Exxon Valdez – BP in The Gulf of Mexico.

Page 45
NOTE 23
When Russia invaded Afghanistan, the mothers of dead soldiers used to argue over nameless graves saying it was their son's.

Page 50
NOTE 24
Myxomatosis. Myxoma virus was introduced into Australia to control the rabbit population, and then to Europe where it spread. Genetic immunity and partial resistance has now developed.

Page 53
NOTE 25
Lowliness – low-pressure area – anti-clockwise circulation of wind.

Page 54
NOTE 26
Ravens have good memories and line up trees to mark where they have left their own food, and where other birds have hidden their food. They are then able to locate it and retrieve it, even if it is some time since they hid it. Celtic people associated ravens with war, death, and the battlefield due to their carrion diet.

Page 55
NOTE 27
Wings behind its back. The Duke of Edinburgh walks with his hands behind his back.

Page 56
NOTE 28
Commemoration Day at the Cenotaph – if a sword, worn below a great coat, goes under the tail it pushes it up.

Page 58
NOTE 29
The solar elevation angle defines how high the sun is.

Page 61
NOTE 30
Trains from the ports in the southeast of England transported the British and American forces that were injured to their respective hospitals. The original flat roofed buildings are still being used by a few hospitals. Training of doctors carried on during the war; when they qualified they had the option to specialise, but many joined the armed forces 'to serve their country'. Surgeons in East Grinstead hospital became experts in plastic surgery, treating many burn injuries. Men had skin grafts to their faces and new noses constructed; some had salvage surgery to their hands, and were left with the stump of a thumb. [6]

Train drivers travelled long distances outside their region, and were transported home by bus to make the same journey after a sleep. The firemen worked non-stop to keep the fire going on long journeys because the quality of the coal was often poor – it was called 'nutty slack'. The crews carried gas masks in case the train ran into a contaminated area. Marshalling yards were targets for German bombers. Train sleeping car corridors were full of members of the armed forces who were being transported to ports in the southeast; their heads on their knees trying to get some sleep. Italian and German POWs, who were transported to towns well away from the bombing, lived in camps. They were ordered to labour, and if this was outside houses they might be invited in, some becoming friendly with the residents; escape for them was pretty nigh impossible with the barrier of the English Channel. Some people who made friends with POWs tried to contact them after the war ended, and a few married.

Wisps of smoke rise from a coal fire, the smell evocative of a steam train – olfactory memory. You remember a situation in the past by association with a smell in the present. When I was a young lad I used to go to watch steam trains shunting. The town was a fishing port and the fishermen tarred their nets (there were no synthetic materials to make nets, and fisherman had to repair them by hand) and hung them out to dry near the trains – the smell of creosote and the smoke from a coal fire is evocative of that time in my life. Boys liked to watch trains (and collect their numbers) because they represented power: the fire, the steam, the hissing, the noise from the open moving parts going faster as the speed increased; a beast waiting at a station to be unleashed. When I was a teenager I used to go to an Italian café and eat ice cream. When I first ate *Häagen-Dazs*, the taste took me back thirty-five years to those times and associated memories – gustatory memory.

Page 64
NOTE 31
Doctrine of choice – RC / C of E / Protestant. Why have there been so many wars between different religions, when religion is about peace and friendship?

Page 68
NOTE 32
Thoughts aligned the tumblers of his mind, releasing the secrets of his soul – a safe's lock.

Page 71
NOTE 33
Electricity – our hearts depend on the force to work; it can stop them beating, but can restart them when they stop beating; the discs insulate humans from the force. The electromotive force is carried in transmission cables at almost the speed of light to produce light and heat. It is generated in a dam by potential hyrdo-static energy, which becomes mechanical energy when the water falls downhill into a turbine, a magnet with a copper stator, and is converted into electricity without pollution. The voltage is raised in transformers to minimise energy loss in conductors, and then dropped at substations to supply consumers.

Page 71
NOTE 34
Lined by poplar trees – in northern France there are many straight roads lined by poplar trees; a metaphor for determination and purpose.

Page 71
NOTE 35
An Egyptian temple was built with its orientation aligned so that the sun entered it only on two days in the year, one in February, and one in October. When the Aswan dam was built this temple was relocated to higher ground, and the sun now enters it one day out of synchronisation. How has this happened with all our technology, when Egyptian engineers could accomplish this three thousand years ago?

The obelisk symbolised the sun god Ra who crossed the heavens. At the end of each day he was thought to die, and sailed on his night voyage through the underworld leaving the moon to light the world above; the next day he was born again.

How many of us think there is something else after death; there is: our souls live on in the memory of those who love us.

One obelisk, a monolith (built from a solid piece of stone), which was transported from Egypt, stands in front of the Vatican. It was originally in a different position but a Pope ordered it to be moved to its present location. The movers faced the death penalty if it was dropped and broken. When it was first erected it was consecrated by exorcism and crowned with a cross. This obelisk, which was the focus of Egyptian paganism, and now stands before the mother of Romanism in St. Peter's square in Rome, is at the centre of a large pagan solar wheel, the symbol of Baal within the symbol of Ishtar, all representing pagan sun worship.

A coin was minted to celebrate the pontificate of John Paul ll. On the reverse side is the sun wheel and obelisk of St. Peter's piazza; distinct rays of sun emanate from the Basilica. Sun entering the dome of St. Peter strikes the hub of the sixteen-ray sun wheel, and Popes wear a stole that bears the pagan symbols of Baal and Shamash with an eight-pointed star of Ishtar. Timothy Youngblood

Page 78
NOTE 36
Spitfire – Literary licence – based on dogfights between a P51 Mustang and a Me109 on Youtube.

Page 79
NOTE 37
ADP is the molecular currency of energy and life, which is produced in mitochondria, the power plants of cells.

Page 80
NOTE 38
An assumption of crocuses, being that the sun would always shine on them.

Trees and flowers capture CO_2, and with the energy of the sun and water make sugars, their food. They give out O_2 in a well-orchestrated balance that has come about through evolution so that we can exist in harmony with their beauty; this equilibrium has changed and we produce too much CO_2 from fossil fuels.

Page 81
NOTE 39
Fountains of tears – underground watering system.

Page 85
NOTE 40
Desert Rats – British 7th Armoured Division in North Africa.

Page 85
NOTE 41
Desert Fox – Rommel.

Page 86
NOTE 42
Dripping – animal fat.

Page 86
NOTE 43
In the Arctic, the red fox is driving out the smaller Arctic fox as a warming climate allows them to survive much further north, and the camouflage of the Arctic fox's white coat is negated. [7]

Page 89
NOTE 44
Aurora Borealis – Northern Lights. They exist, have evolved, and survive because of these inbound dancing atomic forces,

which were marshalled at the dawn of time. The atoms crash into each other and air molecules, and exchange quanta of energy, releasing visible eletcro-magnetism in the form of light of different colours of the spectrum in a technicolour display that guides the swans out of the darkness.

Page 90
NOTE 45
Left – 'sinistra' in Latin – sinister – evil – at the beginning of the 20th century some children were forced to write with their right hands.

Page 90
NOTE 46
Goose – relation of swan. German forces marching – goose-stepping.

Page 92
NOTE 47
Jews and resurrection – most Jews believe in the resurrection of the body after burial, but not from their ashes after cremation. They believe that burial enables the slow separation of the soul from the body, as opposed to the abrupt disengagement and transition to ash by cremation. The soul suffers a shock from the sudden severance, but burial allows it to slowly depart the body and wait for its resurrection.

Father Time, who holds an hour-glass, is married to Mother Earth. The Grim Reaper, the personification of death is married to Life; he conducts souls of the recently dead into the afterlife.

The soul is the seat of the emotional centres of the brain, our personality. People get pleasure from being with us depending on our attitude and behaviour. These centres have developed through evolution so that we survive, balancing love and friendship with aggression. When you die, your soul, your speech and actions, live on in the memory of those who love you – the afterlife; they show that they love you by their speech. The soul eventually dies, your memory fading with time as it is passed down through the generations. But it can be kept alive if you are talked about. Some languages have no written form, only verbal, and speech is the only way to pass memories down with the historical use of people's names.

Page 96
NOTE 48
Swans migrating towards the Arctic.

Further north in the Arctic temperatures are rising, glaciers crumbling, and ice shelves melting to form pack ice; polar bears movements are limited because this type of ice does not support them. As a result, they have less opportunity to catch seals, which do not need to come up through vent holes to breathe. At the other end of the world in the Antarctic tight pack ice prevents penguins getting to the open sea to feed freely. They feed on krill, which eat algae and plankton beneath ice shelves; therefore there is less food available. Loss of sea ice means nesting grounds decrease in size causing a decline in their numbers. This, combined with suction harvesting, threatens them and the ecosystems on which fish, seals, penguins and whales depend. Consequently, penguins have to survive over winter without food, entering it with less body fat and loss of ability to withstand the cold. Krill are believed to be important in removing CO_2 by eating carbon-rich food near the surface, excreting it when they sink down to colder waters to avoid sea predators and albatrosses.

Page 96
NOTE 49
Native American Indian – their conviction that money will be useless to prevent deforestation, poisoning of rivers, and depletion of food resources, which are stealing the wealth of the land, is proving correct, as is their proverb, 'we do not inherit the Earth from our ancestors, we borrow it from our children'.

The prisoners' nightmares were not caught in dream catcher webs (used as a charm by North American Indians to protect sleeping people from nightmares), disappearing with the light of day; their good dreams were not filtered through the webs to slide down the feathers to their sleeper.

Page 97
NOTE 50
Lead – sinker

Page 97
NOTE 51
Sometimes acid, black smuts (from chemical works and iron ore smelting) rain down on their spotless purity, and turn leaves from green to brown. The strident whine of a chainsaw disturbs the silence at the edge of an open area of trees, and a monument to nature crashes down. It damages the branches of trees, and kills surrounding flora and fauna, another depletion of the army that takes in CO_2 and puts out O_2, vital to the equilibrium of the global climate. This deforestation, and subsequent loss of low foliage and roots that prevent eroded soil silting up lakes, river estuaries, and coastlines, affects their ecosystems. Logging of forests accelerates transfer of carbon to the atmosphere by killing trees, which capture and store carbon through photosynthesis, and releases vast amounts

of carbon stored in trees and in the peaty soil below, either through burning, or when timber decomposes.

Page 97
NOTE 52
Rising sun – Japanese flag.

Page 97
NOTE 53
Red is the traditional colour of the Communist movement – 'red sky at morning shepherd take warning' (of bad weather). Line from a mariner's rhyme.

In the USSR, where Stalin committed the state ideology to Marxism-Leninism, repressing elements of the population by creating an atmosphere of political paranoia, and people were persecuted and murdered because of their pursuit of freedom of speech, a bear roars in the wilderness and shakes its head in rage over an oblong pit it had unearthed full of bones with no meat on them. In the gloom the noise of metal breaking stones could be heard.

USSR – Russian Bear (symbol for Russia) – Communism – human rights abuse of their own people. Gulags – hard labour – breaking stones – pit of bones – mass graves.

Page 98
NOTE 54
Vietnam war – Cambodia – Communism – Pol Pot – fields ran red with blood

Page 99
NOTE 55
Bees pick up a positive electric charge when flying. They detect a negative charge on flowers that are rooted to the earth.

When they land on a flower the positive charge is discharged to the earth. Other bees flying by detect there is no charge, indicating there is no nectar, and fly onto another flower saving time and energy when collecting food.

Page 101
NOTE 56
RN – Royal Navy – requiescat navigans – may he be at rest sailing

Page 104
NOTE 57
When the 'Laconia' was sunk by U-156 early in WWII, the commander and crew commenced rescue operations and were joined by crews of other U-boats in the area. Heading to a rendezvous with neutral Vichy French ships under Red Cross banners the U-boats were attacked by an American bomber, despite the Germans informing the allies that they had allied sailors, children and women on board. Hitler was furious when this was reported to him. Subsequently, commanders were ordered (Laconia Order) by Grand Admiral Karl Donitz to stop trying to rescue civilian survivors.

Page 106
NOTE 58
Butterfly flaps its wings – might change the destiny of the world. Chaos Theory – a flap of a butterfly's wings might cause a hurricane in another part of the world.

Page 107
NOTE 59
'Segregated in death' – a nurse, who died in the Second World War, was buried separately in a local cemetery, and facing the men.

Page 107
NOTE 60
SOE – Special Operations Executive.

Page 112
NOTE 61
Lighting up the sky – phenomena of light lasting milliseconds, flash upwards from thunderclouds when an electric field forms above them. These are called elves, red sprites and blue jets, and they are thought to be formed by the injection of high energy electrons created by cosmic rays hitting air molecules. The electrons are repulsed upwards by the same negative charge from the electric field formed by the powerful electro-magnetic pulses generated by lightning discharges. They collide with O_2 and N_2 molecules; energised to higher levels they release radiation in the form of gamma rays, and optical and electro-magnetic emissions. When the quanta of energy dissipate they fall back to two levels, emitting light at opposite ends of the electro-magnetic spectrum; red light where the atmosphere is rarefied, and blue in the lower atmosphere where air molecules are more concentrated.

Page 119
NOTE 62
Sit in nature and be ravaged by it – sunburn.

Sit in nature and be ravaged by it, accelerated by man's ravages – a decrease in the ozone layer increases the amount of UV light entering the atmosphere, which increases the risk of developing skin cancer. Ozone forms in the stratosphere by UV radiation splitting O_2 molecules into O_2 atoms, each oxygen atom joining an O_2 molecule to form O_3 (Ozone). As a result, there is a constant cycle of forming, splitting and reforming of Ozone; UV light absorbed by the process cannot reach Earth.

CFCs that were used in refrigerators and to propel aerosols resulted in more U.V. light penetrating the atmosphere due to thinning of the ozone layer, causing an increased risk of skin damage; these have been phased out. They had only a small effect on ocean temperature; however, although levels are decreasing it will take 40 years to reach 1980 levels.

Man's ravages – in China increasing Carbon Dioxide levels – smog from steel foundries – acid rain – dams flooding villages. Deforestation – pollution of rivers – over fishing – damage to coral reefs. – plastic bags/bottles eaten by fish choking them – nets drowning dolphins and turtles because they can't get to the surface to breathe – glass bottles – flip flops – raw sewage discharge into the sea – oil spills – air/water pollution.

Page 120
NOTE 63
Societies on Earth cannot integrate – countries, even friendly ones (USA and UK) distrust and spy on each other.

Page 120
NOTE 64
Malthus Theory. The population would increase faster than the food supply and a resource limit would be reached (overpopulation). Any further increase might result in famine, disease and war.

Page 120
NOTE 65
Used to have a picnic with her husband – involuntary memory.

Page 121
NOTE 66
'A la recherché du temps perdu' – in search of lost time – remembrance of things past – Marcel Proust – voluntary memory.

Page 121
NOT3 67
Two steps forward and one to the side – knights move.

Page 126
NOTE 68
In Sci-Fi films aliens do not look like us, are depicted as being threatening, and attack us with death rays.

Page 126
NOTE 69
Geneva / Hague conventions
Assassination of a president. JFK wanted to bring a measure of peace to the world – he supported a ban on nuclear weapons testing from 1956 – and end years of racial discrimination and the horrific murder of thousands of black people who were tortured, hung and shot. Black communities are only now airing the extent of the atrocities. Brave men from these communities fought for the United States in WW l, WWII and Vietnam but were still segregated after these wars.

Rules in 'peace' – sectarian wars – genocide – ethnic cleansing – religious extremism – suicide bombers – gun massacres.

The Iraq war – Saddam Hussein – 'The Mother of all Battles' – has spawned many sons of battles.

In the Central African Republic, a large land locked country, Muslim and Christians are slaughtering each other with machetes: who knows when it will end. Islamic extremist groups might find a safe haven, organise terrorist training, and launch attacks from there. French soldiers have already been killed in what will become jungle warfare.

Nelson Mandela has died: let the world rejoice in his life-long sacrifice. He relinquished so much for the freedom of his country; he transcended the categories of skin colour. He was the champion of democracy against the evil of apartheid, his philosophy of life surpassing political boundaries. When he was released after twenty-seven years in jail, he was the personification of magnanimity in triumph, showing no animosity towards his captors, only forgiveness and reconciliation.

The Arab spring – the Arab fall, occurred across North Africa. It was initiated due to numerous factors, including dictatorship, human rights violence, political corruption, poverty and unemployment.

The conflict in Syria is between forces loyal to the government and those seeking to oppose the president because of his one party state and human rights violation. The death toll has now reached 120,000, and both government and opposition forces have committed human rights violation; chemical weapons have been used more than once. More than 2,000,000 Syrians have fled the country and are refugees. Thousands of families are starving to death in freezing conditions. Jihadists, who have been fighting in Syria, are returning to Britain. Do they pose a threat to UK security?

REFERENCES

1. Battles involving soldiers – All Quiet on the Western Front by Erich Remarque.
2. Funerals – Brian Parsons – British Institute of Funeral Directors – The Management of Civilian Funerals in WWII.
3. Stockings – Sarah Sundin – Make it Do – Stocking Shortages in WWII.
4. German War Commemoration Ceremonies. The New York Times May 9th 2005
5. Ravens – 'nostrils covered by bristle like feathers'. Perrins, Christopher (2003) The New Encyclopaedia of Birds. Oxford University Press: Oxford.
   Spatial memory – Clayton, Nicola and Emery, Nathan (2003) 'Corvid Cognition'. Current Biology (15) 3: R80 – R81
   Scarecrow – Shades of Night: The Aviary. Version of 2004 – JUL – 21
6. Train drivers: Bristolian Train Drivers Marc Nussbaumer (permission given)
7. Arctic Fox Hannah, Lee (2010) Climate Change Biology. Academic Press. p. 63

www.ingramcontent.com/pod-product-compliance
Lightning Source LLC
LaVergne TN
LVHW041625070426
835507LV00008B/452